START EACH DAY POSITIVELY RIGHT

There is a saying that the longest journey starts with a single step. Your first step toward wealth, self-improvement, success, and happiness is as simple as opening this book, finding today's date, and embracing a golden tomorrow—you can do it right now.

JANUARY 27: Self-respect is the best means of getting the respect of others.

MARCH 11: Sometimes it is wiser to join forces with opponents than to fight them.

JUNE 4: If it isn't your job to do it, perhaps it is your opportunity.

AUGUST 16: Failure is not a disgrace if you have sincerely done your best.

OCTOBER 22: Your true age is determined by your mental attitude, not the years you have lived.

This complete compendium covers all facets of total achievement the Napoleon Hill way. Never before has it been made so easy to turn your dreams into reality.

NAPOLEON HILL'S POSITIVE ACTION PLAN

THE NAPOLEON HILL FOUNDATION is a nonprofit, charitable organization devoted to imparting Napoleon Hill's philosophy of personal achievement. It now reaches millions of people around the world through the publication of books, periodicals, recordings, and individual study courses, and by sponsoring seminars and study groups.

NAPOLEON HILL'S

P O S I T I V E

ACTION PLAN

*365 Meditations for Making
Each Day a Success*

Interpreted and updated by
MICHAEL J. RITT, JR., AND
S A M U E L A . CYPERT

Preface by
MICHAEL J. RITT, JR.

Introduction by
W. CLEMENT STONE

Edited by
MATTHEW SARTWELL

A PLUME BOOK

PLUME
Published by the Penguin Group
Penguin Books USA Inc., 375 Hudson Street,
New York, New York 10014, U.S.A.
Penguin Books Ltd, 27 Wrights Lane, London W8 5TZ, England
Penguin Books Australia Ltd, Ringwood, Victoria, Australia
Penguin Books Canada Ltd, 10 Alcorn Avenue,
Toronto, Ontario, Canada M4V 3B2
Penguin Books (N.Z.) Ltd, 182–190 Wairau Road, Auckland 10, New Zealand

Penguin Books Ltd, Registered Offices: Harmondsworth, Middlesex, England

Published by Plume, an imprint of Dutton Signet,
a division of Penguin Books USA Inc.
Previously published in a Dutton edition.

First Plume Printing, February, 1997
11 12 13 14 15 16 17 18 19 20

Ⓟ REGISTERED TRADEMARK—MARCA REGISTRADA

The Library of Congress has catalogued the Dutton edition as follows:
Ritt, Michael J.
Napoleon Hill's positive action plan: 365 meditations for making each day a
success / interpreted and updated by Michael J. Ritt, Jr., and Samuel A.
Cypert; edited by Matthew Sartwell.
p.   cm.
ISBN 0-525-93997-0 (hc.)
ISBN 0-452-27564-4 (pbk.)
1. Success.   2. Self-actualization (Psychology)   I. Hill,
Napoleon, 1883–1970.   II. Cypert, Samuel A.   III. Sartwell, Matthew.
IV. Title.
BF637.S8R49   1995
158'.1—dc20   95–18412
                                                        CIP

Printed in the United States of America
Original hardcover design by Steven N. Stathakis

BOOKS ARE AVAILABLE AT QUANTITY DISCOUNTS WHEN USED TO PROMOTE PRODUCTS
OR SERVICES. FOR INFORMATION PLEASE WRITE TO PREMIUM MARKETING DIVISION,
PENGUIN BOOKS USA INC., 375 HUDSON STREET, NEW YORK, NEW YORK 10014.

CONTENTS

v

PREFACE

Napoleon Hill was a man ahead of his time. Although during his lifetime he was recognized as the all-time bestselling motivational author, we are still learning to understand many of the concepts he introduced to us.

His bestseller *Think and Grow Rich!* was first published during the 1930s and has since sold more than 20 million copies in several languages around the world. It is an enduring philosophy. Almost all of his ideas about personal achievement are as applicable today as they were when he first wrote them.

I worked personally with Napoleon Hill from 1952 to 1962 and remained good friends and collaborator with him until his death in 1970. On my wall hangs a handwritten note from Napoleon Hill that says: *To my good friend Michael Ritt, who made priceless contributions to my work during the years of our association.*

We collected 365 Napoleon Hill quotes, epigrams, and self-motivators—one for each day of the year—and organized them into categories that we thought would be most beneficial to you. We then interpreted and analyzed each of the quotes and, in keeping with the Napoleon Hill philosophy, offered suggestions and recommendations for implementing the ideas contained in the messages.

Napoleon Hill firmly believed that in order to help readers gain the most benefit from his works, we should not only tell you what to do, but we should also tell you how to do it. We've attempted to do exactly that in this volume.

To gain the most from this book, read a page each day. Throughout the day, make a concerted effort to apply the principle or the idea contained in that day's message. At the end of the day, set aside a few minutes to evaluate your performance and identify things that you might have done better. Put those ideas into practice tomorrow.

Because of the breadth and depth of Napoleon Hill's philosophy of personal achievement, you may very well find new meaning each time you study his writings. It is my sincere hope that you will continue to find inspiration in his words for years to come as you practice his teachings.

Best of all, if you study and apply the principles he wrote about, only good can come to you. There is nothing in them that is negative or harmful. I hope you find in this book the inspiration and advice that will help you discover the greatness within you, and that one day you will look back upon the purchase of this book as a turning point in your life.

I wish you great success!

—MICHAEL J. RITT, JR.

INTRODUCTION

I can clearly recall, as though it happened only days ago, my first meeting with Napoleon Hill at a luncheon more than four decades ago. I told him how, in 1937, I had been given a copy of his book *Think and Grow Rich!* and found that so many of the principles in it coincided with my own that I sent a copy to each of my sales representatives. The results were fantastic! They were motivated to levels of achievement they once thought impossible.

Near the end of the luncheon, I asked Dr. Hill, "Why don't you come out of retirement and devote five years to finishing your life's work?" His almost immediate response surprised me: "I will . . . if you will become my general manager!"

In the moment that passed before I enthusiastically agreed, two things flashed in my mind: the fact that my time was almost entirely devoted to building my insurance business, and the realization that working with this man would help me achieve my lifetime goal to make this a better world in which to live. For there is a universal law that when you have a goal—particularly a big goal—and you are striving to reach it, and you are sincere in striving to reach it, you will quickly recognize and be ready to accept whatever will help you achieve it.

That meeting marked the beginning of an association that was to last ten years—twice as long as I had originally suggested to him.

We were both willing to devote a decade of our lives to our partnership because we both recognized that inspiration, like enthusiasm, is extinguished unless it is refueled. Just as you need a balanced diet and vitamins to renew your physical body, you need Vitamin I—Inspiration—for the maintenance of a healthy mind and a healthy attitude.

This book contains 365 Napoleon Hill quotations, one for every day of the year. Each quotation is accompanied by an inspirational message that interprets and analyzes Dr. Hill's words and tells you how to apply in your daily life the powerful concepts contained in the quotations. The principles of success that Hill immortalized in his bestselling books have withstood the test of time because they are "actionable." He didn't simply tell us *what* to do; he told us *how* to do it. People around the world have earned great wealth and acquired the true riches of life by applying his philosophy of success.

During the years Dr. Hill and I worked together, we endeavored to change the lives of others for the better by motivating them to learn the proven principles of success and then to follow through with action. I fervently believed then, and I still believe today, that when you employ tried-and-true PMA (Positive Mental Attitude) concepts, not only will you reach the goals you set for yourself—you will also help to make the world a better place.

Regardless of who you are, you are the most important person alive as far as you and your life are concerned. Believe in yourself and build on your positive experiences. Work to develop good and positive characteristics. Focus on them with a white-hot intensity, for it is through the application of PMA principles that you will develop the sincere belief that you cannot fail, that you *will* succeed at whatever you choose to do.

It is also imperative for you to realize that knowledge in itself is not power—it is only *potential* power. You already have unlimited potential power through the marvelous human computer we call a brain and nervous system. In the pages of this book, you will learn how to tap your inner potential and convert potential power into *real power*—through action.

You can make your future what you want it to be if you are willing to pay the price to read, understand, comprehend, and apply the principles contained in this book. The universal principles are few in number and easy to learn; each of the quotations contained herein amplifies and explains one of those fundamental principles. Day by day, week by week, month by month, you can become better and better at applying them by using a formula that works today as well as it did when Napoleon Hill first committed it to writing.

Use these quotations to strengthen your PMA every day. When you make the choice to live life in the positive sense, each step in the right direction brings rewards, some small and immediate, others large and lasting. This book will help you build the momentum you need to achieve the most ambitious goal you may set for yourself. You will be attuned to opportunities that come your way, and you will create opportunities for yourself where seemingly none exist.

You will also learn how to deal constructively with adversity. Successful people realize that we all face adversity in our lives and that those who achieve great success are those who know we can't always control events, but we can control the way we react to them. Instead of accepting a temporary setback as a failure, achievers realize that, as Napoleon Hill said, "In every adversity, there is the seed of an equivalent or greater benefit."

Defeat is never permanent unless you accept it as such. When you live life in the positive sense, you will face adversity with confidence and determination, recognizing that adversity is never permanent. Temporary setbacks become learning experiences that prepare you for success when it eventually arrives. It is that PMA approach to life that will allow you to begin to realize the potential that lies dormant within you.

Use the quotations in this book and the thoughts that accompany them to help you develop good habits and positive character traits and to eliminate negative thoughts and habits. Spend a few minutes each day in thoughtful study, analyzing that day's quotation and reflecting upon its significance in your life. Think about how you can use this information to help you become the person you wish to be, someone who is happy, productive, positive, and successful.

Learn every day from Napoleon Hill's philosophy. We are

all different people with different hopes, dreams, desires, and goals for our lives, but the principles outlined here will benefit everyone who applies them. When you live life in the positive sense, you can earn the income you desire and also accrue for yourself and your family the true riches of life. And you will know that *Whatever you can conceive and believe, you can achieve—with PMA!*

—W. CLEMENT STONE

JANUARY

Traits of Character

1. DEPENDABILITY IS THE FIRST FOUNDATION STONE OF GOOD CHARACTER.

People of character do what they say they will do, when they say they will do it, and according to agreed-upon conditions. They are the leaders, the individuals to whom others turn for guidance because they have demonstrated that they care, that they can be trusted. If you respect yourself enough to keep commitments even when it's inconvenient to do so, others will come to respect you too.

Dependability, like any other character trait, is a habit. Begin today—at the beginning of a new year—to develop the dependability habit. If you procrastinate or find it difficult to meet your commitments, start small. Promise yourself that you will be on time, for example, and manage your time so that you are. Soon you will find that it's easier to keep other commitments as well.

2. YOU CAN TELL BY THE COMPANY PEOPLE CHOOSE WHAT SORT OF CHARACTER THEY HAVE.

As the saying goes, "Birds of a feather flock together." We usually choose friends and business associates who like the same things we do, people who share the same values. If you choose happy, positive, productive companions, the odds are that you are or will soon become happy, positive, and productive yourself. Unfortunately, the reverse is also true. Unhappy, negative, destructive people are sure to drag you down with them.

Choose to spend most of your time with persons who

have PMA—a Positive Mental Attitude. If your job requires you to spend time with negative people, limit that time to the best of your ability and above all don't let them discourage you with their negativism. Instead, display your own PMA.

3. YOUR REPUTATION IS WHAT PEOPLE THINK YOU ARE; YOUR CHARACTER IS WHAT YOU *ARE*.

You want your reputation and your character to match, but concentrate on your character. You may be able to fool others about the kind of person you really are for a time, but it seldom lasts for long. The surest way to make sure your character and your reputation are the *same* is to live your life in such a way that nothing you do would embarrass you if it were printed on the front page of the newspaper. Good character means not ever taking ethical shortcuts, even though everyone else may be doing so. You build good character by doing the right thing because it's the right thing to do.

4. EVERY THOUGHT YOU RELEASE BECOMES A PERMANENT PART OF YOUR CHARACTER.

Thoughts *are* things. Every thought you release—good or bad—is a form of energy that can affect those who receive it, for better or worse. More important, your thoughts affect you. You become what you think about most. If you think about success, you condition your mind to seek success, and you attract large portions of it. Conversely, if you think about failure and despair, you will become miserable and desperate. To keep your mind on a positive track, the moment you begin to experience creeping negativism, make a conscious decision to eliminate negative thoughts and replace them with their positive counterparts.

5. SOUND CHARACTER IS OUR GREATEST ASSET BECAUSE IT PROVIDES THE POWER WITH WHICH WE MAY RIDE THE EMERGENCIES OF LIFE INSTEAD OF GOING DOWN UNDER THEM.

Without PMA, life might be described as long periods of uncertainty punctuated by occasional emergencies that shake you to the very core of your being. The emergencies may be financial, personal, or health related, but each must be dealt with separately and swiftly. The surest way to deal with any crisis is to focus on solutions, not on the probable cause of the problem or who should be blamed for it. Conduct a quick damage assessment, take the time to think through the alternatives and their consequences, and then act to implement the best solution. If you deal with life's emergencies as they occur—on your own terms—you will be a stronger, better person for having looked them in the eye and conquered them.

6. SOME PEOPLE RESEMBLE A CHEAP WATCH. THEY ARE NOT DEPENDABLE.

It would be unrealistic to expect an inexpensive, mass-produced watch to perform with the same degree of accuracy as a finely crafted Rolex. They are not made with the same quality of materials or with the same craftsmanship. Yet we somehow think that we do not need to give the same attention to our most important asset: ourselves.

Don't leave something as important as your character to chance. Choose the character traits you admire, and work to develop them. Don't be discouraged when you stumble. Building character is a process that takes a lifetime to complete. Fortunately, like anything else, the more you work at character building, the better you become at it.

7. PICK OUT SOME PERSON WHOM YOU ADMIRE AND IMITATE HIM OR HER AS CLOSELY AS YOU CAN. THIS MAY BE HERO WORSHIP, BUT IT IMPROVES CHARACTER.

The difference between starry-eyed hero worship and thoughtfully emulating role models lies in the ability to make the distinction between good character traits and ones that may not be so good. Your heroes won't be perfect; none of us is.

Recognize that we are all human, forgive your heroes if they display failings, and continue to emulate the things about them that you like and respect. Comparing your own character to that of others who have achieved great success in their fields broadens your horizons and elevates your goals. When you see what others have done and the character they have developed in the process, you will be able to better recognize how to improve your own performance.

8. BOASTFULNESS IS GENERALLY AN ADMISSION OF AN INFERIORITY COMPLEX.

Really capable people don't have to boast about their achievements; they let their actions speak for them. When you boast about your accomplishments, you are telling others that you are unsure of yourself and your value in the world. Baseball manager Tommy Lasorda once noted that there are those who watch things happen, those who wonder what happened, and those who make things happen. Strive to be one of those who make things happen. If you *show* others what you can do, they will respect you far more than if you had simply told them what you'd done. Anyone can quarrel with words, but actions speak for themselves.

9. PROFANITY IS A SIGN OF INADEQUATE VOCABULARY OR UNSOUND JUDGMENT—OR BOTH.

Mark Twain once observed that "the difference between the right word and the almost-right word is the difference between lightning and a lightning bug." It is never appropriate to use profanity, especially among people you do not know well. Instead, build your vocabulary by reading and studying so that you can express yourself simply and eloquently. When you expand the number of words you know, you also expand your mind, because understanding the words and their meanings necessitates understanding the concepts behind them. Make sure you allow time each day for study and reflection.

10. IF YOU MUST BE DECEITFUL, BE SURE YOU NEVER TRY TO DECEIVE YOUR BEST FRIEND—YOURSELF.

A better understanding of what you are about—your goals, your dreams, and your aspirations—leads you to a better understanding of those around you. It is critical, therefore, that you be honest with yourself at all times. The moment you begin to deceive yourself is the beginning of the decline in your character; it is the beginning of a process of rationalization that permits you to justify unacceptable behavior. Make sure you are a person whom *you* like, a person of sound character. If you don't like yourself, how can you expect others to like you? Step back and examine your behavior as logically as possible. Ask yourself, "Am I the kind of person I would like to be with?" Developing good character traits is like achieving any other objective. Determine where you wish to be and then develop a plan for getting there.

11. MONEY IS EITHER A GOOD OR BAD INFLUENCE, ACCORDING TO THE CHARACTER OF THE PERSON WHO POSSESSES IT.

It's true. Money has no character, no personality, no values. Its actions only reflect the desires of its owner. Money can build great hospitals and schools, or it can be gambled away or squandered on meaningless possessions. Money may build museums to house beautiful works of art, it may construct beautiful houses of worship—or it may be used to create instruments of war and destruction.

As you build your personal wealth, make sure you build your character by setting aside a portion of your income to help others. Choose a church, a charity, or a cause that you can enthusiastically support. Then give of your money and your time in support of that cause. The primary beneficiary of such noble actions is always the one who gives, not the one who receives.

12. NO ONE IS SO GOOD THAT HE HAS NO BAD IN HIM, AND NO ONE IS SO BAD THAT HE HAS NO GOOD IN HIM.

We human beings are a complex lot. Many religious writings and great literary works are based upon the constant struggle between good and evil that goes on inside every one of us. This struggle is as old as mankind itself. Yet, while we recognize our own inner struggles, we are often quick to condemn others. Psychologists tell us that there is no such thing as a bad person; there are only bad behaviors.

Make it a point to look for the good in yourself—and in others. Nurture the good character traits and work on the ones that may need improvement. Like plants in a garden, the character traits that grow strong and productive will be those that are fed, watered, and weeded regularly.

13. THE PERSON WHO IS HONEST ONLY FOR A "PRICE" SHOULD BE RATED AS DISHONEST.

There are no degrees of honesty. There are only absolutes. Either you are honest or you are not. Honesty does not come for a price; honesty is its own reward. It's also the most efficient form of human behavior. Honest persons never have to worry about which lie they have told to whom, and they never have to worry about getting caught. Thus, they are free to focus all their energies on more productive things.

Make it a habit to be honest in all your dealings. If you can't be truthful in what you say, don't say anything at all. Remember, small lies start out innocently enough but soon assume lives of their own. A small lie requires a larger one to conceal it, and soon more, even larger lies are required. Don't tell that first lie or take a single thing that doesn't belong to you, and you'll never have to worry.

14. A LAZY INDIVIDUAL EITHER IS SICK OR HAS NOT FOUND THE WORK HE OR SHE LIKES BEST.

No one is inherently lazy. It is human nature to want to be doing things unless we are ill. A sure sign of the beginnings of a recovery from illness is the desire to get up and around, to go back to work, to do something—anything. Inactivity leads to boredom, and boredom leads to "laziness." Conversely, activity leads to interest, and interest leads to enthusiasm and ambition.

W. Clement Stone often says, "The emotions are not always subject to reason, but they are always subject to *action*!"

Determine what you are best at and what you like to do, and develop a burning desire to be the best you can be at it. Then get into action!

15. IF YOU HAVE SOUND CHARACTER, YOU WILL FIND THAT YOU GENERALLY DO NOT WORRY ABOUT YOUR REPUTATION.

Thomas Jefferson once said that a majority is one man with the courage of his convictions. If you have the courage that comes from the sincere conviction that you are a person of sound character, an honest, dependable, kind, and caring person, you will never have to worry about what others think of you. If you know in your own heart that you are a good and decent person, you can meet life's challenges head-on and without fear of what others think.

16. ATTEND WELL TO YOUR CHARACTER, AND YOUR REPUTATION WILL LOOK OUT FOR ITSELF.

Most of us at one time or another have been misunderstood by those who are important to us. They thought we planned to take an action they disliked when in truth our intentions were to proceed in an entirely different direction. Such misunderstandings are usually quickly righted and life goes on. The same is true with character and reputation. If your reputation is for some reason misaligned with your character, it will soon quickly right itself when others discover for themselves that you are not at all the kind of person they had assumed you were.

If your foundation is strong, you never need to be concerned about such misunderstandings. Others will learn soon enough what kind of person you really are. Spend your time and energy in constant self-inspection and self-improvement, building strong character, and you will never have to worry about what others think of you.

17. FALSEHOOD DOES EVERMORE HAVE A WAY OF PUBLISHING ITSELF.

It is virtually impossible to conceal the truth forever. It is the natural order of things that the truth will eventually come out. This single fact is the foundation of our judicial system and the basis on which all human relationships are formed. A business, professional, or personal relationship built upon a lie cannot long endure, but one that is founded on truth and equality of benefit for the participants is unlimited.

Make it a practice to tell the truth in all that you do—even when it doesn't matter—and you will form a habit of truthfulness. You will know instinctively that it is better to tell the truth and face the consequences than to launch a falsehood that will eventually make itself known to the world.

18. YOU ARE EITHER HONEST OR DISHONEST. THERE CAN BE NO COMPROMISE BETWEEN THE TWO.

Officials who deal with fraud and theft say they are often amazed at the small amounts of money some people will steal. Some people will sell their integrity for a pittance. To those individuals, dishonest behavior is not an occasional occurrence—it is a way of life. Those who lie about insignificant things or steal trivial amounts of money will develop the habit of lying and stealing.

As you look back on your own behavior, can you do so with pride in the knowledge that you have always been honest? If you cannot, perhaps it is time to think about the times when you chose dishonest behavior. Why did you do it? Was it worth it? Wouldn't the consequences of being honest and truthful have been far better in those circumstances? Learn from your mistakes and vow that from this day forward you will always be honest.

19. BANKERS OFTEN LEND MONEY ON CHARACTER, BUT SELDOM ON REPUTATION ALONE, FOR THEY HAVE LEARNED THAT NOT ALL REPUTATIONS ARE DESERVED.

When considering a loan, a banker attaches great importance to three things: the borrower's ability to repay the loan, the borrower's credit history, and the borrower's character. The first two considerations can be calculated mathematically; the third requires judgment and experience. Prudent bankers have learned that persons of character are always a good risk because they take their obligations seriously while those who spend their resources on the trappings of success should be avoided at all costs.

Protect your good reputation as you would protect your home, your investments, and your life. Once shattered, a good reputation can only be regained by those who have developed the courage and willpower to persevere in the face of great odds.

20. HONESTY IS A SPIRITUAL QUALITY THAT CANNOT BE EVALUATED IN TERMS OF MONEY.

There are many practical reasons to practice honesty. It requires far less effort to be truthful than to be deceitful, and in the long term the risks are fewer and the rewards greater. But in today's complex society, the boundaries of acceptable behavior have been blurred until they are sometimes indistinguishable. Laws and codes of ethics establish *minimum* standards of behavior. Make sure you establish standards for yourself that exceed such minimums, a standard below which you will not allow yourself to fall, regardless of what others may do or say. Your own set of standards will allow you to decide quickly and easily upon an appropriate course of action when faced with a difficult problem.

21. IT'S MIGHTY EASY TO JUSTIFY DISHONESTY IF YOU MAKE YOUR LIVING FROM IT.

The subconscious mind makes no moral judgments. If you tell yourself something over and over, your subconscious mind will eventually accept even the most blatant lie as fact. Those whose lives and careers have been destroyed by dishonest behavior began the process of self-destruction when they convinced themselves that one slight infraction of the rules wouldn't matter. When you sell yourself on an idea, make sure the idea is positive, beneficial to you, and harmless to others. Just as negative thoughts and deeds return to their originator, so do positive ones. When you practice honest, ethical behavior, you set in motion a force for good that will return to you many times over.

22. TOO MUCH TRUTH WILL MAKE SOME PEOPLE MADDER THAN TOO LITTLE.

Schoolchildren sometimes play a game called "Honesty." The rules are simple: For a designated period of time, the participants must tell the truth regardless of the subject. They then ask each other leading questions such as, "Do you like my hair?" "Do you think Lindsay is cute?" Inevitably someone gets angry when he or she discovers that these friends had been shading the truth, telling "little white lies," to spare the person's feelings. Even when the game is over, its lessons are not soon forgotten.

Being honest with others doesn't mean being brutal. It

isn't necessary to tell people everything you don't like about them under the guise of being frank with them "for their own good." Sometimes it's better if we don't know every person's innermost feelings about us. Respect for another's self-esteem often means telling them too little truth instead of too much.

23. POLITENESS USUALLY BEGINS AT HOME OR IT DOESN'T BEGIN AT ALL.

Politeness to others is usually born out of respect for the individual, which you learn as a child. When you are treated with respect by other members of the family, you learn to respect them as well. The self-esteem that results from being recognized as a unique person by the people who matter most to you helps you develop the confidence necessary to succeed later in life. Politeness and consideration for others are habits that—once developed—usually stay with you for a lifetime. While common courtesy may seem relatively insignificant in the grand scheme of things, it is a reflection of more basic values. More important, if you develop the habit of respecting others, you are likely to command respect from them.

24. THE INDIVIDUAL WHO HAS TIME ONLY FOR GOSSIP AND SLANDER IS TOO BUSY FOR SUCCESS.

Each of us has a finite amount of time, energy, and money; you must choose for yourself how you will spend them. If you elect to squander your resources by demeaning others in an attempt to advance your own interests, you will soon find that so much of your time and energy has been spent on gossip and slander that you have little time left for yourself. If you deal in malicious information, you'll rarely be trusted. As the saying goes, "Those who talk about others to us will talk about us to others."

25. GREAT ACHIEVEMENT IS BORN OF A STRUGGLE.

"Our strength grows out of our weakness," said Ralph Waldo Emerson. "Not until we are pricked and stung and sorely shot at, awakens the indignation which arms itself with secret forces." Strife and struggle can inspire you to overcome adversity and to propel yourself to real achievement. View every struggle as an opportunity for personal growth. It is the struggle itself, not the result, that builds character. If you know you are right, stay the course even though the whole world seems to be against you and everyone you know questions your judgment. When you prevail—and you eventually will if you stick to the job—they will all tell you that they knew all along you could do it.

26. DON'T LOOK TO THE STARS FOR THE CAUSE OF YOUR MISFORTUNES. LOOK TO YOURSELF TO GET BETTER RESULTS.

There are many things you cannot control, but you can control the only things that really matter: your mind and your attitude. External forces have very little to do with success. Those who program themselves for success find a way to succeed even in the most difficult of circumstances. Solutions to most problems come from one source and one source alone: yourself.

Living life to the fullest is a lot like shooting the rapids in a rubber raft. Once you've made the commitment, it's difficult to change your mind, turn around, and paddle upstream to placid waters. But it's the excitement and adventure that make it all worthwhile. If you never make the attempt, you may never know the depths of despair, but neither will you experience the exhilaration of success.

27. SELF-RESPECT IS THE BEST MEANS OF GETTING THE RESPECT OF OTHERS.

Have you known people who can't stand to be alone for any length of time? The chances are good that those folks don't like themselves very much. They need others around constantly to validate their own existence. Sadly, the people who need others the most are usually those whom others least like to be around. Because they don't like themselves, other people seldom do either. The surest way to command the respect of others is to become a person *you* like being around. Identify the characteristics you admire in others and make a conscious effort to develop them yourself. Your self-respect begins to grow the moment you decide to take the first step toward becoming the kind of person you know you can be.

28. SOUND CHARACTER BEGINS WITH KEEN SELF-RESPECT.

No one really knows for sure how we develop self-respect, but the experts believe it begins at a very early age. Parents who show their children that they love them unconditionally—just because they are who they are—build a foundation of healthy self-respect that will sustain the children for the rest of their lives. From this foundation comes the moral and ethical structure known as character.

Healthy self-respect should not be confused with egotism. An egotist loves himself for the most superficial of reasons, while a self-respecting person takes pride in qualities of character that he or she has worked hard to develop.

29. IF YOU HAVE MORE ENEMIES THAN FRIENDS, THE ODDS ARE A THOUSAND TO ONE YOU HAVE EARNED THEM.

Abraham Lincoln once observed, "You may fool all the people some of the time; you can even fool some of the people all the time; but you can't fool all of the people all the time." Regardless of how cleverly you package yourself, others will eventually see through your masquerade and recognize you for what you really are. As a general rule, people will accept you for what you say you are until you prove yourself to be otherwise. Don't take advantage of the goodwill of others. Make friends, not enemies.

30. A MOST BENEFICIAL USE OF TIME IS SILENT MEDITATION, WHILE SEARCHING FOR GUIDANCE FROM WITHIN.

We all experience rare moments when a blinding revelation comes to us, when we suddenly see things differently than ever before. Usually, however, we learn the truth about ourselves gradually, over long periods of time, from quiet introspection. We are all spiritual, but some of us have learned to tap more effectively into the great strength that resides in the spiritual portion of ourselves.

The spirit is not boisterous and noisy. Getting in touch with your spiritual self demands tranquillity and solitude. Make sure you dedicate a portion of every day to thought and study, to think and reflect upon your life. Choose a time and place that best allow you to relax your mind and devote your thoughts to reflection.

31. WHEN YOU GET YOURSELF UNDER COMPLETE CONTROL, YOU CAN BE YOUR OWN BOSS.

We all have moments when we allow others to cause us to react emotionally, especially in anger. Often we regret our response later, and we vow we will never allow ourselves to behave in this fashion again. The next time you feel the anger rising, remind yourself that no one can make you angry or emotional without your consent—indeed, your active participation is required.

Those who have learned to manage themselves are the individuals who are destined to be leaders. They are chosen to manage others because they have demonstrated that they can manage themselves. They are people of character.

FEBRUARY

Personal Initiative

1. THE BEST JOB GOES TO THE ONE WHO CAN GET IT DONE WITHOUT PASSING THE BUCK OR COMING BACK WITH ALIBIS.

We often discover that people we view as "overnight successes" have in fact labored for years in obscurity before they were finally recognized and rewarded for their contributions. Success is a cumulative effort; the journey to the top in any field is usually long and requires careful planning.

If you want to climb the first rung on the ladder of success, you must always take the initiative to get the job done, even when you find it less than challenging or even unpleasant. Eventually, you'll earn your reward. You will become the boss, the leader, because you have developed the habit of taking the initiative to get the job done. You will get the best jobs because you've proven that you are dependable by accepting responsibility for your actions and your future.

2. ACT ON YOUR OWN INITIATIVE, BUT BE PREPARED TO ASSUME FULL RESPONSIBILITY FOR YOUR ACTS.

One of the primary differences between those who achieve great things in their lives and those who manage only to "get by" is that successful people learned early in life that they were responsible for their own actions. No other person can make you successful or keep you from achieving your goals.

Taking the initiative means assuming a leadership role, a position that singles you out for praise—and for criticism. The good leader is the one who shares the credit for success with others and assumes full responsibility for failures or temporary setbacks. When you accept responsibility for your actions, you gain the respect of others and are well on the way to creating your own future.

3. WHATEVER STIFLES PERSONAL INITIATIVE IS DEFINITELY AN ENEMY OF INDIVIDUAL ACHIEVEMENT.

Large organizations—including business, government, and the military—are increasingly discovering that their attempts to standardize procedures and centralize decision-making have created a bureaucracy that stifles innovation and initiative. As a result, they are losing ground to leaner, more autonomous operating units that encourage individual initiative.

A culture that discourages prudent risk-taking and affixes blame instead of solving problems will surely eradicate mistakes—because nothing will be done! Innovation means trying and failing and trying and succeeding. Seldom is a winning idea perfect when it's first introduced. A culture that encourages people to take the initiative and try something new nurtures individual and group achievement.

4. HIGH WAGES AND THE CAPACITY TO ASSUME RESPONSIBILITY ARE TWO THINGS THAT BELONG TOGETHER.

It's been said that a leader's job is to inspire others to high levels of achievement, while a manager's job is to protect the assets of investors. The most successful people are those who recognize the similarities and differences between leadership and management responsibilities, fulfilling both with equal skill and aplomb. When they do, they realize the rewards that are commensurate with their efforts.

When you cheerfully accept responsibility for your own actions and do your job in a way that protects the interests of your employer, you will soon be entrusted with more and more responsibilities. And those who have the capacity to assume responsibility—for the success of the project or organization— will always be paid the highest salaries.

5. IF YOU DO A JOB ANOTHER'S WAY, HE OR SHE MUST TAKE THE RESPONSIBILITY. IF YOU DO IT YOUR WAY, YOU MUST TAKE THE RESPONSIBILITY.

The "loneliness at the top" that senior officials often feel comes from the certain knowledge that they alone are responsible for the failure or success of the organization. They may share their authority with associates, but not their responsibility. When a sports franchise suffers a losing season, the general manager and the coaches are held accountable. They, not the individual players, are responsible for the failure of the team; the team merely followed orders. When you become the leader, when you set the course, you must accept responsibility for the outcome.

6. BIG PAY AND LITTLE RESPONSIBILITY ARE CIRCUMSTANCES SELDOM FOUND TOGETHER.

It is possible to go through life without ever accepting any responsibility, but such freedom from the cares of the world comes at an enormous financial cost. If you make it a practice to go out the back door when responsibility walks through the front, you will also miss out on the opportunities that always accompany responsibility. In almost any vocation, profession, or calling, your remuneration is directly proportional to the responsibility that accompanies your position.

Make it a practice to volunteer for more responsibility or simply to assume it. There are times when you must get on with the task at hand without ever being formally told you're in charge of it. If you demonstrate that you are a can-do kind of person, responsibility and the higher pay that accompanies it will come to you.

7. THE PRIVILEGE OF BRINGING CHILDREN INTO THE WORLD CARRIES WITH IT THE RESPONSIBILITY OF TEACHING THEM THE FUNDAMENTALS OF SOUND CHARACTER.

One of life's greatest joys is the sense of wonder that accompanies the arrival of a tiny new human being into the world. But that joy is accompanied by a tremendous responsibility that perfectly encapsulates the need for personal initiative. You can provide children with all the physical advantages of a good childhood, but unless you strive to set a good example for them to follow, you will know only dismay as they reach adulthood and blossom into purposeless drifters.

Your personal initiative, whether or not you are raising a child, must always incorporate exemplary behavior. You cannot take ethical shortcuts, big or small, without other people observing them and assuming that this behavior is something you wouldn't mind having turned back on yourself. Certainly you will make mistakes, but if you have always striven for the best course, others will remember it and treat you accordingly.

8. DON'T COVET THE OTHER FELLOW'S JOB IF YOU ARE NOT PREPARED TO ACCEPT THE RESPONSIBILITY THAT GOES WITH IT.

How often do you look at those around you and say, "I could do any of their jobs better than they can if I only had the opportunity," never realizing the price they have paid and the knowledge they have accumulated to earn the right to hold that position? It's easy to be a Monday-morning quarterback and second-guess the actions of others. But it's far more productive to recognize the contributions of others and give them the credit for a job well done. If you aspire to a higher level of recognition, demonstrate to others—your peers as well as your superiors—that you can be counted upon. The world's greatest rewards accrue to those who always deliver on their promises.

9. LOAFING ON YOUR JOB HURTS YOUR EMPLOYER, BUT IT HURTS YOU MORE.

Some people expend far more energy getting *out* of work than they would spend doing the job well. They may think they are fooling the boss, but they are only fooling themselves. An employer may not know all the details of every job or every task an individual performs, but a good manager knows the *results* of effort. You can be sure that when promotions or plum assignments become available, they won't be offered to loafers.

If you do your job cheerfully and well, not only are you more likely to be recognized and rewarded, but you also learn how to do your job better. As you become more proficient, you become more valuable to your employer. You also acquire the most valuable of all assets—the confidence that comes from knowing you possess skills that will increase your value to any organization.

10. THE PERSON WHO WORKS HARDER WHEN THE BOSS ISN'T AROUND IS HEADED STRAIGHT FOR A BETTER JOB.

It is a foregone conclusion that you will never reach great heights of success if you perform at high levels only when others are watching you. The most exacting standards of performance should be those you set for yourself, not those set by others for you. When your expectations for yourself are higher than your boss's expectations for you, you will never have to worry about job security. If you work to *your* highest standards, the promotions will take care of themselves.

11. IT TAKES MORE THAN A LOUD VOICE TO GAIN RESPECT FOR AUTHORITY.

Margaret Thatcher once observed that being powerful is like being a lady: If you have to tell others you are, you aren't. Truly great leaders gain respect by the way they conduct themselves, not by the loudness of their orders. You gain respect by respecting others. Follow the Golden Rule in your treatment of others, and you will win their undying loyalty.

If you ever expect to have authority over others, you must first prove yourself worthy. You must demonstrate to them that you care about them, that as their leader you will always look out for their interests. A good officer always makes sure the troops are provided for before he takes care of his own needs. It's a lesson that all too often is lost in the scramble to get to the top—but one that will most certainly undercut your progress if you overlook it.

12. OVERCAUTION IS AS BAD AS NO CAUTION. IT MAKES OTHER PEOPLE SUSPICIOUS.

If you expect others to have confidence in you, you must conduct yourself in a way that inspires trust. Being so cautious that you never try anything new will damage your credibility just as much as will throwing all caution to the winds and trying any idea that comes along without thinking it through. (Most people equate any kind of extreme behavior with poor judgment.) But don't fall victim to "analysis paralysis." Learn to separate facts from opinions and make sure your decisions—

and your subsequent actions—are based on reliable information. Then take action!

13. THE PERSON WHO COMPLAINS THAT HE OR SHE NEVER HAD A CHANCE PROBABLY HASN'T THE COURAGE TO TAKE A CHANCE.

Thomas Edison once observed that the reason most folks don't recognize opportunity when it comes along is that it is often dressed in coveralls and looks like work. Often opportunity involves a great deal of work and a willingness to take a chance on something, the outcome of which may be uncertain.

Eventually you reach a point when you must either accept an opportunity with all of its unknowns or else turn your back on it. No one can tell you when you have reached that point; you alone know when it's time to make your move, to have the courage to take a chance.

14. A BLIND BOY PAID HIS WAY TO A MASTER'S DEGREE AT NORTHWESTERN UNIVERSITY BY TAKING NOTES ON CLASS LECTURES IN BRAILLE, TYPING THEM, AND SELLING COPIES TO CLASSMATES WHO HAD STRONGER EYES BUT WEAK AMBITION.

One of the great mysteries of life is why some people who seem to have all the advantages—the right connections, education, and experience—never seem to amount to much while others who have had to struggle for everything they have reach incredible heights of success. It hinges on determination. If you have the will to succeed, you will somehow find a way, regardless of the obstacles you encounter.

Do you use all of your assets to achieve your goals, or are you handicapped by your lack of ambition? No other person can create in you a desire to succeed. With enough motivation, you will see things all around you that will help you reach your objectives, things that you may have overlooked many times before.

15. IF YOU BECOME DISCOURAGED, THINK OF HELEN KELLER, WHO, THOUGH SHE WAS DEAF, DUMB, AND BLIND INSPIRED HER MORE FORTUNATE CONTEMPORARIES THROUGH HER BOOKS.

The life of Helen Keller is an outstanding example of the triumph of the human spirit over a physical handicap. Even today, decades after her death, her life stands as a beacon of hope for those who must constantly struggle just to perform routine tasks that most of us take for granted. Whenever you feel fate has been unkind to you, all you must do is look around you and you will begin to appreciate how fortunate you are. Make sure your life's plan includes giving something back to the community without expecting anything in return. Giving time and effort, not just money, reinforces your connections to your community, provides you with concrete proof of the effectiveness of deliberate action, and reminds you of the inspiring power of determination in human endeavor.

16. IF YOU START AT THE TOP, YOU CAN MOVE IN ONLY ONE DIRECTION—DOWNWARD.

Perhaps the worst thing that might have happened to you would be to have been born with the proverbial silver spoon in your mouth. For had you been born into privilege, you would have been deprived of one of the world's greatest gifts: the opportunity to reach the highest levels of success of which you are capable, solely on the basis of your own merit. If you were born with less than most, don't resent others who seem to have more advantages. In truth, the real advantage is yours, for you will develop the self-confidence that comes only from meeting life's challenges on your own terms. As you progress, you gain the strength and knowledge necessary to assure your enduring success, things that cannot be given to you, but must be earned.

17. YOU DON'T HAVE TO DO MORE THAN YOU ARE PAID FOR, BUT YOU CAN PUSH YOURSELF AHEAD MIGHTY FAST BY DOING IT *VOLUNTARILY*.

Initiative is that exceedingly rare quality that prompts—no, impels—a person to do what ought to be done without being told. It's also a commodity upon which the world places great value. Initiative will immediately set you apart from the competition, whether you are an entrepreneur, a professional services provider, a corporate staffer, or an hourly worker. Your boss, your clients, or your customers will notice you and come to depend upon you because you have shown yourself to be a person who can be counted upon always to do the right thing.

18. PROCRASTINATION IS THE BAD HABIT OF PUTTING OFF UNTIL THE DAY AFTER TOMORROW WHAT SHOULD HAVE BEEN DONE THE DAY BEFORE YESTERDAY.

For an achiever, perhaps the most dangerous, most destructive habit of all is procrastination, for it robs you of your initiative. When you put things off once, it's easier to put them off again, until the habit is so firmly ingrained that it cannot be easily broken. Sadly, the effects of the habit of procrastination are also cumulative. Its cure is obvious—action. You'll be surprised how quickly you begin to feel better about yourself and your situation when you get going on something—anything.

As British prime minister and author Benjamin Disraeli said, "Action may not always bring happiness; but there is no happiness without action."

19. THE HABITUAL PROCRASTINATOR IS ALWAYS AN EXPERT CREATOR OF ALIBIS.

If you are so inclined, you can always find dozens of reasons why something can't or shouldn't be done—and precious few why it should or could. It is far easier to rationalize that it's too difficult, too expensive, or too time-consuming than to accept the idea that if we are willing to work hard enough, smart enough, and long enough we can accomplish anything. Instead of making a commitment, we make up an alibi. If you find that you frequently invent excuses for why you didn't do something or have a million reasons why something didn't work out as planned, it's time for a reality check. Stop explaining and start doing!

20. THE TWO KINDS OF PEOPLE WHO NEVER GET AHEAD ARE THOSE WHO DO ONLY WHAT THEY ARE TOLD AND THOSE WHO WILL NOT DO WHAT THEY ARE TOLD.

It's hard to say which would be more discouraging: drifting from job to job because you're always the first to be laid off, or laboring in monotonous obscurity at the same job. The first results from not doing what you are told to do, the second from doing *only* what you are told to do. You can "get by" for a time following either approach, but you will never get ahead. Personal initiative is more important in today's enlightened, high-tech workplace than it was during the Industrial Age, when the ability to follow orders was a critical skill. As technology makes many supervisory functions obsolete, every one of us is expected to do more with less, determine what needs to be done, and do it. Don't wait to be told. Know your company and your job so well that you can anticipate what needs to be done—then do it!

21. FIND OUT HOW TO GET PRODUCTION UP, AND IT WILL DRAG YOU AND A BIGGER PAYCHECK ALONG WITH IT.

It's common knowledge that the person who knows the most about how to improve the productivity of any job is the person who holds that job. Why is it, then, that we are often reluctant to offer suggestions for improvement? Perhaps we've seen too many layoffs and reorganizations to trust the cracker-barrel wisdom that our goal should be to work ourselves out of a job—so that we can move on to a bigger and better position.

Nevertheless, the old wisdom is still sound. If you find a way to do things better, faster, or cheaper, you increase your value to your employer. You will be asked to participate in planning sessions and quality circles because you've demonstrated that you know how to make things work more efficiently. It's inevitable that you will be promoted, because you will become one of those exceptional employees who are too valuable to lose.

22. SAVE EXPENSE FOR THE COMPANY, AND THE COMPANY WILL SAVE MONEY FOR YOU IN PROPORTION.

The rewards may not come today, next week, or even next year, but they will come. When you make it a practice to look after the company's assets as you would look after your own, you have shown that you are worthy of the trust of your employer—and your fellow employees. You are destined for bigger and better things. The savings need not be large. It's the habit of eliminating waste and searching for opportunities to save money that's important. Make it a practice to examine everything you do to see how it could be done more economically, and it is inevitable that you will soon find yourself in charge of larger budgets and more people.

23. IF YOU WORK AS HARD AT THE TASK YOU DESIRE TO DO AS THE TASK YOU MUST DO, YOU WILL GO PLACES.

It's been said that you should always work at two jobs simultaneously: the one you have and the one you desire. When you work as hard at the task you want to do as the task you must do, you are preparing yourself for the future. You are learning skills that will enable you to grow beyond your present position and into your boss's job and your boss's boss's job. When the time comes, you'll be ready.

When you've mastered one task, don't rest on your laurels. Instead, begin immediately to think about the future, about how you can improve what you're doing now, and what you can learn that will allow you to progress in the future. Ours is a knowledge-based economy in which intellectual property is worth far more than physical goods. To succeed today requires continuous learning; staying current in your field means a lifetime of study in our fast-paced world.

24. IN A WELL-MANAGED BUSINESS, ALL PROMOTIONS ARE SELF-MADE. THE EMPLOYER'S ONLY PART IN THE TRANSACTION IS TO CHECK CAREFULLY TO MAKE SURE THE PROMOTION WAS EARNED.

The perfect formula for destroying morale in any organization is to create a working environment that leads employees to believe that the only way to get ahead is by playing politics. The best-managed businesses are those in which every promotion is earned and every qualified person has an equal opportunity to compete for it. If you're a manager, weigh all decisions involving your employees on the basis of fairness. And if you aspire to be a manager, choose to work for a company that is fair in its treatment of workers. When you've earned your position, through skill and effectiveness, you have the best job security.

25. THE GREATEST CURE KNOWN FOR LONELINESS, DISCOURAGEMENT, AND DISCONTENTMENT IS WORK THAT PRODUCES A HEALTHY SWEAT.

Emotions are sometimes strange, volatile, and unpredictable. They do not always respond to logic and reason. They *do*, however, respond to action. If you have occasional feelings of loneliness, discouragement, or discontentment, the best way to kill such negative emotions is to work them to death. Almost nothing is as bad as it first seems, and there's nothing like a hard day's work to put everything in proper perspective.

When you begin to feel negative emotions, dwelling on your misfortunes only makes you feel worse. Do your best to put them out of your mind and think about more positive, constructive things. Physical labor can help. Choose a task that doesn't require a great deal of concentration, and then focus on accomplishing the task at hand.

26. NO ONE CAN KEEP YOU DOWN BUT YOURSELF.

Have you ever felt that sometimes you are your own worst enemy? We all have moments when, no matter how hard we try, things just don't seem to work out right, when everything goes wrong, and we have no one to blame but ourselves. But, just as you may sometimes be your own worst enemy, you can also be your own best friend. The transition usually occurs when you realize that the only person on earth who can determine your failure or success is you yourself.

You may discover your best friend when you develop the maturity and strength of character to accept yourself for the person you are and to take the actions necessary to become the person you wish to be. When you analyze yourself objectively, you can begin to build upon your strengths and compensate for your weaknesses. When you do, you will realize that the only person who stands in the way of your success is you.

27. ARE YOU WAITING FOR SUCCESS TO ARRIVE, OR ARE YOU GOING OUT TO FIND WHERE IT IS HIDING?

The poet John Milton's words "They also serve who only stand and wait" may be both profound and genuine, but the true riches of life are far more likely to accrue to those who actively go out and seek them. Seldom does success come marching in accompanied by a brass band in full regalia. More often, it's achieved by those who labor long and hard.

Take the initiative, and you will create your own opportunities. There is no substitute for action backed up by a well-thought-out plan.

28. IF YOU WERE YOUR OWN EMPLOYER, WOULD YOU BE ENTIRELY SATISFIED WITH THE DAY'S WORK YOU HAVE DONE TODAY?

At the end of the day, it matters little what others think of you; what's important is what you think about yourself. As you reflect on your day's work, ask yourself, Have I given 100 percent of my time and talents today? If this were my company, would

I like it to be filled with hundreds of other people just like me, or would I prefer to hire individuals with a little more initiative?

When you have become the kind of person *you* would like to work with or have working for you, you aren't far from the day when you will own the company—or at least become a valuable part of it. Most important, you can sleep soundly at night, serene in the knowledge that you have done your best, that you have earned your pay, and that you have met the standards of performance you require of yourself.

29. DO IT NOW!

This phrase is the great self-starter, the reminder you need whenever you feel procrastination creeping up on you. (And if procrastination is moving fast enough to find you, you're already at a standstill.)

There are always things that need doing. If you are in the grip of laziness, turn to the first thing you see and set to work. It doesn't matter what it is; what's important is that you break the habit of doing nothing. On the other hand, if you're avoiding a specific chore, then that's the one you need to start acting on right away. Otherwise, that job will continue to grow in your mind as something that is too unpleasant to do. If you make "Do it now!" a habit, you will have mastered the essence of personal initiative.

MARCH

A Winning Attitude

1. THE QUALITY AND QUANTITY OF THE SERVICE YOU RENDER, PLUS THE ATTITUDE WITH WHICH YOU RENDER IT, DETERMINE THE AMOUNT OF PAY YOU GET AND THE SORT OF JOB YOU HOLD.

The people who are promoted to the best positions in the company are those who make it a practice to go the extra mile, to do more than they are paid to do, and to do it willingly and cheerfully. You take the first important step toward determining your own future when you make the conscious decision to approach every task with a positive outlook and to stick with the job until it is done.

If you find this attitude difficult at first, you'll discover it eventually becomes part of you. And after you begin to realize the benefits that accrue to you because you are known as someone who always gives a little extra, you wouldn't consider doing things any other way.

2. THE INDIVIDUAL WITH A NEGATIVE MENTAL ATTITUDE ATTRACTS TROUBLES AS A MAGNET ATTRACTS STEEL FILINGS.

It is a curious fact of nature that somehow our minds find a way to transform into physical reality the things we think about most. If you expect to fail, you can be sure that you will, and if you find something negative in every opportunity, nothing will ever work out positively for you. Fortunately, the reverse is also true. If you are a happy, positive person, you will attract positive things.

You can keep your mindset positive by eliminating negative thoughts the moment they begin to creep into your conscious mind. If you dwell on the negative aspects of every opportunity, you will never accomplish anything worthwhile. Be prudent about the risks you take, but don't be paralyzed by fear of failure.

3. IF YOU ARE WORRIED OR AFRAID OF ANYTHING, THERE IS SOMETHING IN YOUR MENTAL ATTITUDE THAT NEEDS CORRECTION.

Worry and fear are negative emotions that serve no useful purpose. Worse, they are not benign influences on your behavior. Both tend to expand if left unchecked until they crowd out positive emotions and beliefs, taking over your mind and filling it with counterproductive emotions that cause you to doubt your ability to succeed at anything you attempt. Unless you control worry and fear, one day you will discover that they control you.

While the emotions can't always be corrected with logic or reason, they are always susceptible to action. Act, and even if your actions aren't entirely appropriate for the situation, the very act of doing something—anything—constructive will have a positive effect on your mind and attitude.

4. REMEMBER THAT NO ONE IS EVER REWARDED OR PROMOTED BECAUSE OF A BAD DISPOSITION AND A NEGATIVE MENTAL ATTITUDE.

If you really examine any well-managed organization, you will find that the people who are most successful are those who are positive and helpful, people who always find the time to offer encouragement and praise when it is deserved. The people who occupy the top positions are almost always happy, enthusiastic people who encourage others to behave in the same way. Yet there are always a few individuals who never seem to get the message and behave as though they can complain their way to the top.

There isn't a single situation in your career, your relationships with others, or in your personal life that benefits from a negative attitude. All will be greatly improved if you make it a practice to approach life in a positive way.

5. QUICK PROMOTIONS ARE NOT ALWAYS THE MOST ENDURING.

Most people who fail after receiving a promotion do so because they fail to rise to the challenges the new position offers. It is perfectly normal to feel a twinge of insecurity when you assume a new position—after all, you've never had this job before—but seldom do promotions come before you are ready for them. Now, it is a fact that the day you are promoted, you are not yet competent in that position. You were promoted into the position because of your *potential*, not because you were expected to perform flawlessly from the outset. Work to prove that your boss's faith in you was justified. Make becoming as proficient as possible in your new job—in the shortest possible time—your number one priority.

6. TRYING TO GET WITHOUT FIRST GIVING IS AS FRUITLESS AS TRYING TO REAP WITHOUT HAVING SOWN.

The Bible states that we reap what we sow. The most fertile soil in the world is barren unless seeds have been properly planted, cultivated, and nurtured. The relationship between giving and getting is constant in everything you do. To succeed in any endeavor, you must first invest a generous portion of your time and talents if you expect ever to earn a return on your investment. You have to give before you get. It's all a matter of attitude. You may occasionally be disappointed if you are not rewarded for your efforts, but if you demand payment for your services before you render them, you can expect a lifetime of disappointment and frustration. If you cheerfully do your best before asking for any compensation, you can expect a bountiful harvest of the greatest rewards life has to offer.

7. IT IS ALWAYS BETTER TO IMITATE A SUCCESSFUL MAN THAN TO ENVY HIM.

Of all the negative emotions, envy is perhaps the most insidious. It is especially sinister because it destroys you from the inside by replacing all that is positive and productive with negative feelings of anger, jealousy, and despair. But when you congratulate others upon their successes and genuinely wish them well, not only do you give credit to those who deserve it, but you also feel better about yourself. Once you've overcome your envy, you may want to determine what specific actions the other person took to achieve success. Meanwhile, you will have strengthened your relationships by recognizing the achievements of others.

8. IT IS ALWAYS SAFE TO TALK ABOUT OTHERS AS LONG AS YOU SPEAK OF THEIR GOOD QUALITIES.

The old adage "If you can't say something nice about someone, don't say anything at all" is especially valid today. In any organization, regardless of size, the rumor mill works overtime when it comes to negative gossip. And you can be sure that unkind things you say about others will very quickly find their way to them, for it is also a truism that those who talk about others to us talk about us to others. Not only should you not speak badly of others—you should not participate in conversations in which others do. Spend your time with those who focus on important things, and you will never have to apologize for an unkind word uttered in a moment of weakness.

9. YOU EITHER RIDE LIFE OR IT RIDES YOU. YOUR MENTAL ATTITUDE DETERMINES WHO IS "RIDER" AND WHO IS "HORSE."

There is no compromise or negotiation when it comes to who will run your life. Either you take charge and live a productive life of your choosing or you allow yourself to be ruled by circumstances. But there will inevitably be setbacks. In the old West, a cowboy expression went: "There never was a horse that couldn't be rode, and there never was a rider that couldn't be throwed." Like everyone else, you will have days when everything goes right and you are on top of the world. Relish those days, enjoy them, and remember them. Recall the euphoria that accompanied them when you need an extra measure of positive thinking to get back in the saddle after you've experienced an embarrassing and painful fall.

10. INSTEAD OF COMPLAINING ABOUT WHAT YOU DON'T LIKE ABOUT YOUR JOB, START COMMENDING WHAT YOU DO LIKE AND SEE HOW QUICKLY IT IMPROVES.

It's easy to find fault with any job. Whatever your occupation or profession, there are always some unpleasant and mundane tasks you would rather omit. It is also easy to allow the things you dislike to dominate your thoughts and for you to overlook the fact that the things you dislike about your work are really a very small percentage of the overall job. Make it a point to find something good in your job every day. It need not be a big, important event; simply finding joy in doing one thing particularly well will suffice. Then, instead of looking forward to the end of the day, you will find yourself actually looking forward to *going* to work.

11. SOMETIMES IT IS WISER TO JOIN FORCES WITH OPPONENTS THAN TO FIGHT THEM.

What a better world this would be if we worked together in harmony toward the achievement of our shared goals instead of engaging in petty disputes and turf battles. When you allow yourself to be dragged into personality conflicts, game playing, arguments about who gets the credit, and disagreements about trivial issues, they only drain your energy and sour your attitude. Plus you waste valuable time that could be spent on far more important matters.

When you make an effort to understand others' motivations, you may well discover that your opponents have far more in common with you than you think. When you cage your ego and look at the situation from the other person's point of view, you can almost always find a way to work together for your mutual advantage.

12. NO ONE COULD RIDE A HORSE IF THE HORSE DISCOVERED ITS REAL STRENGTH. THE SAME THING IS TRUE FOR PEOPLE.

Horses are massive, gentle creatures who are by far larger and stronger than the men and women who handle them, yet they docilely obey the commands they are given. It doesn't seem logical that a large, powerful animal would allow itself to be mastered by a human being, yet we have been able to use our intelligence to dominate the animal kingdom. You can use these same forces to allow the positive side of yourself to dominate the negative. A Positive Mental Attitude allows you to tap the source of great power that resides within you, enabling you to accomplish things you never before believed were possible.

13. IF YOU HAVE MORE ENEMIES THAN FRIENDS, IT'S TIME TO EXAMINE YOUR MENTAL ATTITUDE.

When your enemies outnumber your friends, the answer to the problem most likely resides within you. Ask yourself, Am I the kind of person I would like to have as a friend? Do I consider the feelings of others, or do I think only of myself? Do I try to find the good in others, or am I always finding fault? When something goes wrong, do I search for a solution to the problem, or do I look for someone to blame? In the answers to such questions, you may find the answer to the question: Why do I have more enemies than friends?

14. YOUR MENTAL ATTITUDE DETERMINES WHAT SORT OF FRIENDS YOU ATTRACT.

If you want to be a positive, successful person, be sure you choose your friends carefully. Positive friends and role models will have a positive effect upon you, while negative friends will soon kill your initiative. Do not allow yourself to be lulled into complacency by the masses who believe mediocrity is an acceptable alternative. Focus on the possibilities for success, not the potential for failure. When you doubt yourself, talk the situation over with a positive, supportive friend. Everyone needs a boost now and again; make sure your friends are positive, success-oriented people who always build you up, not negative thinkers who always seem to find a way to tear you down.

15. BEFORE TRYING TO MASTER OTHERS, BE SURE YOU ARE THE MASTER OF YOURSELF.

When you develop a Positive Mental Attitude, you immediately set yourself apart from the crowd. You become a leader because positive thinking leads to positive action, while negative thinking leads to apathy and inaction. When you take the initiative in any situation, others will follow simply because they like to associate with people who know where they are going. In order to lead, however, you must first be willing to discipline yourself. The first rule of leadership is never to ask others to do what you are unwilling to do yourself. You can lead only by example. Being a leader requires you to work harder and longer than the others and proving you are the master of your own destiny.

16. THE BEST RECOMMENDATION IS THE ONE YOU GIVE YOURSELF BY RENDERING SUPERIOR SERVICE— WITH THE RIGHT MENTAL ATTITUDE.

What others think of you is important, as long as it coincides with what you think of yourself. If you are recognized by others as a positive person who always makes an important contribution, you will be in demand, for there are never enough such people in any organization. Your co-workers will value you, your customers will appreciate you, and your boss will recognize and reward you if you stick with it. You may not become an overnight success, but neither will you fail instantly and permanently. Make it a habit to go the extra mile with a Positive Mental Attitude.

17. CHARACTER IS ACCURATELY REFLECTED IN ONE'S MENTAL ATTITUDE.

Without a strong foundation built on positive character traits, success will not long endure. It is virtually impossible to fake good character. Phonies are quickly spotted because they haven't the substance and determination to maintain the charade. Developing good character begins with a positive attitude. Your desire to be a good, decent, honest, considerate person must first take place in your mind. When you make the decision to become a person of character, you will also find that you are much more willing to do the right thing simply because it is the right thing to do.

18. A NEGATIVE MIND SPAWNS ONLY NEGATIVE IDEAS.

It is a physical impossibility for a negative mind to generate positive thoughts. When you allow yourself to dwell on the negative aspects of life, negative thinking expands to fill all of your thoughts until there is no room for positive thoughts to grow. It becomes an endless cycle. The habit of negative thinking generates more and more negative thoughts, which the mind attempts to turn into physical reality. The result is a life of despair and hopelessness. Develop the habit of eliminating negative thoughts the moment they appear. Start small at first. When you first hear that inner voice that says, "I can't do this," put the thought out of your mind immediately. Instead, concentrate on the task itself. Break it down into manageable parts and complete them one at a time. When the job is finished, tell your doubting self: "You were wrong. I could do it, and I did!"

19. IT DOESN'T PAY TO LOOK AT OTHERS THROUGH A FOGGY MENTAL ATTITUDE.

You must keep your mind sharply focused on your goals, and you must have a grounding philosophy that sustains you when the going is tough. When you apply the principles of success consistently until they become a part of you, no longer will you have to stop and think about what you should do in any given situation. Your positive response will be automatic.

Make sure you spend time in reflection and study. Clearly establish your goals and develop a plan and timetable for their achievement. Read the works of motivational writers and the great philosophers, and use the knowledge you gain to develop your own code of conduct. Establish your own philosophy of success that you can stick with—day in and day out —regardless of what the rest of the world does.

20. A POSITIVE MENTAL ATTITUDE IS AN IRRESISTIBLE FORCE THAT KNOWS NO SUCH THING AS AN IMMOVABLE BODY.

Time and again we hear stories about ordinary people who do seemingly impossible things when they find themselves in an emergency situation. They perform herculean feats of strength and endurance, things they never dreamed they were capable of doing. Wouldn't it be wonderful if you could harness that strength and make it available anytime you need it? You can —if you believe you can.

No doubt you can remember a time in your life when you were exceptionally focused on your objective, a time when you achieved more in less time than ever before. Perhaps it was an impending vacation that motivated you to get everything done before you departed, or perhaps it was a "must pass" exam that helped you focus your concentration. The intensity that you developed in those situations is always available to you when you have a Positive Mental Attitude.

21. REMEMBER, YOUR MENTAL LIMITATIONS ARE OF YOUR OWN MAKING.

For years, athletes attempted to run a mile in four minutes but it seemed to be a barrier that no one could overcome. Then on May 6, 1954, a British runner named Roger Gilbert Bannister ran a mile in 3:59.4 minutes to establish a world record. Soon afterward, other runners broke Bannister's record. Too often, we accept conventional wisdom as fact. Make sure you set your goals high enough. Don't settle for less because of limitations you place upon yourself. Most of us never really reach the level of achievement of which we are capable because we don't challenge ourselves to do so. Perhaps Robert Browning said it best: "A man's reach should exceed his grasp,/Or what's a heaven for?"

22. IF YOU ARE SURE YOU ARE RIGHT, YOU NEED NOT WORRY WHAT THE WORLD THINKS.

If you are ever to achieve noteworthy success in your life, you must be willing to stand apart from the crowd. Success is something that is achieved by the minority, not the majority, of people. You will also discover as you climb the ladder of success that there are many who, out of jealousy or envy, will belittle your achievements. Nevertheless, if you have the courage of your convictions, nothing can deter you from your course. You develop confidence in your beliefs by doing your own thinking and by constantly testing and revising your knowledge. Use W. Clement Stone's R^2A^2 Principle to Recognize and Relate, Assimilate and Apply information from any field to help solve your problems and direct your thinking.

23. MOST ILLNESS BEGINS WITH A NEGATIVE MIND.

It's been proven again and again. Hypochondriacs, people who are convinced that they are sick even though nothing is wrong with them, experience the exact symptoms of the actual illness. For them, the illness is just as real as if their bodies were ravaged by disease. It is also possible to make yourself ill through constant worry and fear of failure, because the mind constantly strives to turn into reality the things we think about most. Protect your mental health with the same care you give your physical body. Just as your body requires healthy, nourishing foods, and a balanced diet, so does your mind. Make sure you feed it plenty of positive thoughts.

24. INDIVIDUALS WITH POSITIVE MENTAL ATTITUDES ARE NEVER FOUND IN A RUT.

Individuals with a positive attitude are those who somehow always manage to find something new and interesting even in the most mundane tasks. They don't allow themselves to be bored, because they are always seeking ways to do things faster, better, and more efficiently. If you make it a practice to find better ways to do the same old things, you will soon be marked for advancement. You will be supervising others who are performing your old job because you've proven that you are a person who can be counted on to take the initiative and do what needs to be done without being told.

25. IF YOU ARE AN AMERICAN CITIZEN, DON'T LET ANYONE TELL YOU THAT YOU ARE DOWNTRODDEN.

We still live in the greatest country in the world. The United States is the great experiment in positive thinking; our entire system of government is based upon faith in the inherent goodness of the individual. It was a revolutionary idea more than 200 years ago when the Declaration of Independence was first signed. Borrowing from the greatest thinkers in history, our founding fathers established a form of government of the people that is today the model most imitated around the world. Economic and political conditions ebb and flow, but as long as we have a democratic society that celebrates the individual, we can achieve anything in life we desire. All you require to be successful in the United States is the desire to achieve success and the determination to stick with it until you reach your goals.

26. IT ISN'T DEFEAT, BUT RATHER YOUR MENTAL ATTITUDE TOWARD IT, THAT WHIPS YOU.

There are many things in life that you cannot control, but you can always control your attitude toward them. Defeat is never permanent unless you allow it to be so. When you have a positive attitude, you will recognize failure for the impostor that it is and realize that it is really a learning experience, a valuable lesson that will help you succeed with the next attempt.

Ask yourself: What could I have done differently that would have altered the outcome? What can I do in the future to minimize problems and mistakes? What did I learn from this experience that I can put to good use next time? If you approach obstacles and setbacks with a positive attitude, you will be surprised how quickly you can turn defeat into victory.

27. IF YOU HAVEN'T THE WILLPOWER TO KEEP YOUR PHYSICAL BODY IN REPAIR, YOU ALSO LACK THE POWER OF WILL TO MAINTAIN A POSITIVE MENTAL ATTITUDE IN OTHER IMPORTANT CIRCUMSTANCES THAT CONTROL YOUR LIFE.

A Positive Mental Attitude is not developed in a single decision to replace negative thoughts with their positive equivalent. It is a sustained commitment that requires personal discipline, the same kind of discipline that is required to stay in shape and maintain your physical health. It is a commitment that must be reinforced daily, or it is soon forgotten and cast upon the scrap heap of good intentions. When you take charge of your fate and determine that you will live positively in every aspect of your life—physical and mental—you will receive an extra benefit. Positive physical conditioning will reinforce your Positive Mental Attitude, and your positive attitude will help you stay in better physical condition.

28. YOUR OWN MENTAL ATTITUDE IS YOUR REAL BOSS.

While your time and your labor may be subject to the demands of your employer and others, your mind is the one thing that cannot be controlled by anyone but you. The thoughts you think, your attitude toward your job, and what you are willing to give in exchange for the compensation you are paid are entirely up to you. It is up to you to determine whether you will be a slave to a negative attitude or the master of a positive one. Your attitude, your only master in life, is entirely within your control. When you control your attitude toward events, you control the eventual implication of those events.

29. A MIND ILL WITH NEGATIVE ATTITUDES IS MORE DANGEROUS THAN A SICK BODY, FOR ITS SICKNESS IS *ALWAYS* CONTAGIOUS.

Experts in human behavior have discovered that it is virtually impossible for an individual member of a group not to be affected by other members. Likewise, the group itself is only as strong as its weakest link. It is rarely possible for the entire group to raise itself to higher levels of achievement than that of which the weakest member is capable. It is only possible for individuals who break out of the group to exceed the potential of the group as a whole.

Don't associate with those who are afflicted with the mental sickness of constant negative thinking. Associate with happy, positive, productive people. Your time is an asset to be managed more carefully than your money; spend it with people who share your desire to succeed and your commitment to maintain a Positive Mental Attitude.

30. KEEP YOUR MIND FIXED ON WHAT YOU WANT IN LIFE, NOT ON WHAT YOU DON'T WANT.

We have just begun to explore the inner workings of the mind, but we have long been aware of the effects of our thoughts. When you focus on not missing the target instead of on hitting the bull's-eye, the results are often disastrous, for it is impossible to think negative thoughts in a positive way. Ask any golfer who has tried not to miss a putt or a bowler who has struggled not to miss a strike.

Make sure your goals are specific and precise. "Making a lot of money" or "earning regular promotions" are wishes, not goals. State exactly how much money you expect to earn and when, and the specific promotion you want, how you plan to earn it, and when you expect to do so. As Carlson Companies chairman Curt Carlson once noted, "Obstacles are those frightening things you see when you take your eye off the target."

31. CHANGE YOUR MENTAL ATTITUDE, AND THE WORLD AROUND YOU WILL CHANGE ACCORDINGLY.

Your world will become what you choose to make it. You can reach great heights of success, or you can settle for a miserable life that is devoid of hope. The choice is yours. When you choose a positive course, you set in motion an unstoppable force that will allow you to have a fulfilling career, the love of your family and friends, good physical and mental health, and all of the other true riches of life.

To change your world, you must change it from the inside out. You must begin with yourself. When you choose the course that puts your life on a positive track, you will change your life for the better, and you will also positively influence the people with whom you come in contact.

APRIL

Goal-Setting

1. YOU CAN DO IT IF YOU BELIEVE YOU CAN.

It's called a "self-fulfilling prophecy" when something occurs because we believe it will. The mind is constructed so that it constantly seeks to bring into physical reality the things it thinks about most. Most of us will never realize the tremendous potential we possess—because we are unwilling to believe that we can accomplish things that others believe are impossible. "Impossible" jobs require more effort and greater concentration, but when they are completed, the rewards—both financial and psychic—are commensurate with the effort required. You may not be able to achieve everything you'd like, but you won't accomplish anything unless you believe you can.

2. YOU COME FINALLY TO BELIEVE ANYTHING YOU TELL YOURSELF OFTEN ENOUGH— EVEN IF IT IS NOT TRUE.

If you repeat something over and over to yourself, your subconscious mind will eventually begin to accept it as fact. When something has been accepted as truth by your subconscious mind, it will work overtime to transform the idea into physical reality. You can take advantage of this by programming your mind to think positive thoughts. Use self-motivators or affirmations to persuade your subconscious that you are capable of doing anything you wish. Repeat the self-motivator several times a day until it becomes an automatic reaction to recall a positive phrase whenever you begin to doubt yourself. Replace "I can't" with *"I will!"*

3. IF YOU DON'T BELIEVE IT YOURSELF, DON'T ASK ANYONE ELSE TO DO SO.

It is virtually impossible not to transmit your doubts and insecurities to others through body language, tone of voice, inflection, word choice, and other subtle characteristics. When you show by your actions that you lack self-confidence, other people also begin to doubt your ability to perform. You can gain the respect and confidence of others. Begin by making a list of all the things you like about yourself and the things you would like to change. Make a conscious effort to build upon your positive strengths and correct your weaknesses. It may not be easy, but if you assess yourself objectively and persevere in your efforts, you will eventually prevail.

4. MIGHT THROWS ITSELF ON THE SIDE OF THOSE WHO BELIEVE IN RIGHT.

We human beings are the only creatures on earth who have the capacity for belief. That capacity, combined with our almost innate capability to distinguish right from wrong, provides us with a formidable power in our quest for a richer, more rewarding life. When you set goals for yourself, make sure they are based on doing the right thing for your family, your friends, your employees, and yourself. When others see that you are fair and just in your dealings with them and that you are a generous, principled person, they will move heaven and earth for you.

5. THE CON MAN WORKS HARDER AND PAYS MORE FOR WHAT HE GETS OUT OF LIFE THAN ANY OTHER PERSON, BUT HE KIDS HIMSELF INTO BELIEVING HE IS GETTING SOMETHING FOR NOTHING.

There is a fundamental rule in sales: You must sell yourself first before you can effectively sell others. If you don't believe in the value of your products or service, no one else will either. If you are conning others into an unfair deal, you must work mightily to overcome your internal resistance to doing something wrong. A deal is a good one only when it is good for everyone involved. When each participant has an equal opportunity to profit and the risk is shared among partners who care about one another's welfare, not only is the likelihood of success far greater, but the journey toward it will also be much more enjoyable.

6. WHO TOLD YOU IT COULDN'T BE DONE, AND WHAT GREAT ACHIEVEMENTS HAS HE PERFORMED THAT QUALIFIED HIM TO SET UP LIMITATIONS FOR YOU?

You will find as you go through life that those who give advice most freely are precisely the individuals who are least qualified to do so. Busy, successful people don't have an interest in telling you how to live your life. They are busy living their own. Failures or mediocre people have all the time in the world. They also delight in seeing you fail, and are quick to say "I told you so" when you experience a temporary setback.

If someone tells you that what you are attempting to achieve is impossible or not worth the effort, take a close look at them and what they have accomplished with their lives. The chances are good that you will find they haven't done much. Successful people are *optimistic* people. They have the habit of success because they learned long ago to listen to themselves and not to those who would like to see them fail.

7. WHERE WILL YOU BE TEN YEARS FROM NOW IF YOU KEEP ON GOING THE WAY YOU ARE GOING?

Many people fail to realize that big success is the result of little successes achieved, often over a very long period of time. Truly successful people are long-term thinkers. They know that they must build upon each achievement and constantly learn new and better ways of doing things. A regular review of your progress is an essential part of goal-setting. A goal is little more than a wish unless it has a timetable for completion. Make sure your plan for your life includes short-, medium-, and long-term goals. Revise your goals as circumstances dictate, check them off when they are completed, and set new and bigger goals for yourself as you grow. And take time to reflect often to make sure you are on the right course—for you.

8. NEVER TEAR DOWN ANYTHING UNLESS YOU ARE PREPARED TO BUILD SOMETHING BETTER IN ITS PLACE.

This rule applies to both individuals and things. It's easy to criticize other people thoughtlessly for their shortcomings, and equally easy to find fault in their work or in situations that are not to your liking. It is far more difficult to be a builder of people and to create works of art, useful products, or profitable businesses. Make sure you are a builder, not a destroyer of people and things.

When you criticize the actions or work of others—your children, your employees, or others for whom you are responsible—make sure your criticisms are positive and directed at the act, or the opportunity for improvement, *not* the individual.

Include specific suggestions for their application and focus on the potential for success.

9. WHAT DO YOU WANT FROM LIFE AND WHAT HAVE YOU TO GIVE IN RETURN THAT ENTITLES YOU TO IT?

There is a law of physics that states: For every action, there is an equal and opposite reaction. The same is true in life. You get out of it what you put into it. When you are generous with your time and effort, the rewards will be bountiful. When you give grudgingly, the payback will also be commensurate with your investment. Large returns require large commitments of personal or financial capital.

Understand from the beginning that there is a price tag attached to everything. When you set a goal for yourself and determine that the time, effort, and personal discipline required to achieve it constitute a fair bargain, you will find that even the most ambitious goals are within your reach.

10. THE SUCCESSFUL MAN KEEPS HIS MIND FIXED ON WHAT HE WANTS IN LIFE—NOT ON WHAT HE DOESN'T WANT.

It is virtually impossible not to become what you think about most. If you concentrate on something long enough, it becomes part of your psyche. Use this knowledge to your advantage. If you think about problems, you will find problems. If you think about solutions, you will find solutions. It's normal to have doubts, fears, and insecurities. The successful person understands this and learns to overcome them by focusing on the desirable objective, not on undesirable distractions.

11. YOU WILL GET WHAT YOU WANT IF YOU REFUSE TO ACCEPT ANY SUBSTITUTES.

Compromise is an essential element of politics, diplomacy, and negotiation, but not in setting and reaching goals. People who achieve great success in life are those who are unwilling to accept less than their best from themselves and refuse to compromise on the achievement of their most important goals.

When you find yourself thinking about accepting less than the full measure of what you would like to achieve, stop for a moment and analyze the situation. Are the obstacles you face really insurmountable, or is there another way to attack the problem? Can you go around the obstacle? Any step in the right direction, however small it may seem, will keep you moving toward your goal. Progress toward the achievement of big goals is often measured in inches.

12. NEVER MIND WHAT YOU HAVE DONE IN THE PAST. WHAT ARE YOU GOING TO DO IN THE FUTURE?

Shakespeare's observation that "What's past is prologue" is especially appropriate in today's high-speed, high-tech world. Everything we have done in the past serves only to prepare us for the next task. Don't revel in past glories. Plan for future achievements, and savor the victories of today. Take pride in everything you do, search for better ways to do routine tasks, and congratulate yourself when you do something especially well.

13. THE ONLY PERMANENT THING IN THE ENTIRE UNIVERSE IS WHAT YOU SET UP IN YOUR OWN MIND.

It is true that most of our limitations are self-imposed. We believe that certain things are impossible because we've convinced ourselves that they are. In one experiment, scientists placed a glass divider between two fish, one of which preyed on the other. At first, the predator banged against the glass repeatedly, but eventually it gave up. After a time, the researchers removed the glass divider, but the fish continued to swim benignly in their respective sections.

We, too, are creatures of habit. Make sure you test your boundaries occasionally. As you grow and develop and become better at what you do, you may find that things that once limited you no longer do. Spend some time occasionally in productive daydreaming, considering what you would do if you could do anything you wished. You may find that your dreams are within the realm of possibility when you establish definite, measurable goals and have a plan for achieving them.

14. IF YOU DON'T KNOW WHAT YOU WANT FROM LIFE, WHAT DO YOU THINK YOU WILL GET?

The great majority of people in the world drift through life, never realizing that their future will be the one they create for themselves. The minority who achieve great success are people who know what they want and have a plan for realizing their objectives. They know what they want and how they are going to get it. Your goals should be specific, they should be measurable, they should have a deadline for their achievement, and they should be divided into manageable pieces. Know exactly what you plan to achieve, when you plan to achieve it, and how. Review your progress regularly, correct your course when necessary, and never, never give up.

15. BE SURE ABOUT WHAT YOU WANT FROM LIFE AND DOUBLY SURE OF WHAT YOU HAVE TO GIVE IN RETURN.

Examine the lives of successful people, and you will find that they have paid a price that is in direct proportion to the amount of success they have earned. Close examination will almost always reveal years of study and preparation before great success is achieved. This principle is consistent in virtually every field of individual achievement—in the arts, medicine, science, or business. Nothing worthwhile ever comes easily.

As you consider your own goals, also consider what you are willing to sacrifice for what you expect to receive. You should be prepared to give generously of your time and talents long before expecting a return on your investment. Many "overnight successes" labored in obscurity for many years before they were finally recognized for their achievements.

16. EXAMINE MOST CAREFULLY THE THINGS YOU DESIRE MOST.

Far too many people spend more time planning their weekends than their lives. Then they suddenly realize that life has passed them by and they weren't even aware it was happening. When you intently study what you most desire in life, you begin to focus your mind and concentrate your energy upon that which you wish to achieve. One of the great advantages of having a definite goal for your life is that it helps you prioritize your activities. When your major purpose is clear in your mind, it is unnecessary to analyze each individual situation. You know automatically whether your actions will move you toward your goal or away from it. You can then use all of your resources—time, money, and energy—to best advantage.

17. WISDOM CONSISTS IN KNOWING WHAT NOT TO WANT AS WELL AS WHAT TO WANT.

Your goals should also be designed to create rewards that are most important to you, not to someone else. Some experimentation may be required, particularly during your early years, to find what you really like and what you're best at. Career and financial goals should be balanced with personal goals such as maintaining relationships with people who are important to you. Your plan for your life should also include some fun goals, doing something simply because you enjoy doing it. Spiritual development is also important in becoming a happy, well-rounded person. Make sure you allow time for all important aspects of your personal development.

18. DON'T BE AFRAID TO AIM HIGH WHEN CHOOSING YOUR LIFE'S GOAL, FOR NO MATTER HOW HIGH YOU AIM, YOUR ACHIEVEMENTS MAY FALL BELOW IT.

Many businesses today advocate "continuous improvement" as part of their quality programs. They have realized that to remain competitive in today's global economy they must constantly strive to improve every aspect of the business, otherwise they will be overtaken by the competition. The same ethic applies to individuals. All of life is a continuous learning experience. Every success and every temporary setback only serve to prepare you for the time when you will eventually prevail. Your short- and medium term goals should be realistic and achievable, but your long-term goals should always far exceed your present capabilities. As the Roman poet Virgil said, "Fortune sides with him who dares."

19. IF YOU DON'T KNOW WHAT YOU WANT, DON'T SAY YOU NEVER HAD A CHANCE.

The people who complain the loudest about never having an opportunity in life are usually the ones who always have a ready excuse for their failures. Nothing is ever their fault; they are victims of their heritage, their environment, insufficient education, or any number of other factors that they perceive as placing them at a disadvantage. If you look hard enough, you can always find reasons for not attempting something or not sticking with the job to the end. Successful people, though, are not excuse-makers. They take responsibility for their actions, they set goals, and they assume responsibility for their achievement. Where others see despair, they see hope. They approach every situation with enthusiasm, confident in the knowledge that nothing is impossible for those who have a Positive Mental Attitude.

20. THIS IS A FINE WORLD FOR THE PERSON WHO KNOWS PRECISELY WHAT HE OR SHE EXPECTS FROM LIFE AND IS BUSY GETTING IT.

We are happiest when we are striving to achieve a goal. When we achieve one goal, it's a natural human tendency to set another, usually bigger, one. W. Clement Stone calls it inspirational dissatisfaction—the letdown one experiences after a goal has been achieved and before the next step toward a new one has been taken. When you begin to experience that nagging feeling, it's time to get into action! Make sure you have a long-range plan in place so that when one short-term goal has been achieved, there is a natural progression toward the next.

21. A PERSON WITHOUT A DEFINITE MAJOR PURPOSE IS AS HELPLESS AS A SHIP WITHOUT A COMPASS.

If you analyze a navigator's chart in minute detail, you will find that the trip from one point to another is more a collection of zigzag lines than a straight line from the point of departure to the final destination. The captain makes constant course corrections to account for changes caused by external conditions that cause the ship to stray from its course. The only thing that doesn't change during the voyage is the destination.

The same is true with individuals. Whatever your ultimate plan for your life may be, you will find that there are always environmental influences over which you have no control. Correct your course and continue on toward your destination. The secret is always to have a destination in mind and not to drift with the current.

22. A BURNING DESIRE TO BE AND TO DO IS THE STARTING POINT FROM WHICH THE DREAMER MUST TAKE OFF.

Many years ago, the commencement speaker at a prestigious university asked all members of the graduating class who had a definite plan for their lives to hold up their hands. As he looked around the room, only three hands were raised. Twenty-five years later, when the class held a reunion, the combined net worth of those three individuals exceeded that of the remainder of the class.

People who know where they are going always achieve far greater levels of success than those who merely drift through life, expecting circumstances to create opportunities for them. Successful people create their own opportunities by focusing on goals with an intensity that borders on obsession. In this way, every action moves them toward their goal.

23. WILLPOWER IS THE OUTGROWTH OF DEFINITENESS OF PURPOSE EXPRESSED THROUGH PERSISTENT ACTION, BASED ON PERSONAL INITIATIVE.

Envious people sometimes attribute success primarily to luck. Nothing could be more wrong. As coach Darryl Royal once observed, "Luck is what happens when preparation meets opportunity." Success occurs when you have a definite purpose for your life and you take the initiative to follow through with action. You may make mistakes occasionally—everyone does—but any action is far better than doing nothing.

24. A RUDDERLESS SHIP AND A PURPOSELESS PERSON ARE EVENTUALLY STRANDED ON DESERT SAND.

The goals you set for yourself—like the rudder of a ship—will guide you toward your destination, and without them, like a ship without a rudder, you'll find it impossible to stay the course.

Make goal-setting a habit in your life. If you sometimes have trouble staying focused, set small, attainable goals and stick with the job until it's done. Examples might include finding a faster, more efficient way to do a routine job. Or taking the most difficult jobs first when you have the most energy and your concentration is at its highest level. Save the easiest jobs for last. A few small successes will inevitably lead to bigger achievements.

25. HONESTY AND HARD WORK ARE COMMENDABLE TRAITS OF CHARACTER, BUT THEY WILL NEVER MAKE A SUCCESS OF THE PERSON WHO DOES NOT GUIDE THEM TOWARD A DEFINITE MAJOR PURPOSE.

Character is an important element of success and a critical attribute of leadership, but character alone cannot ensure success unless it is channeled in a positive direction. When good, decent people—persons of character—connect with a major purpose for their lives toward which they willingly and enthusiastically direct their energies, the results can be awe-inspiring. A major purpose and outstanding character are a formidable combination.

26. LIVING WITHOUT A DEFINITE MAJOR PURPOSE PROMISES NOTHING BUT A SCANT LIVING.

You may get by in life without a Definite Major Purpose, but you will never get ahead. Definiteness of purpose is the starting point of all achievement. Financial goals in particular should be specific, definite, and measurable. You should know what you plan to earn, by when, and how you plan to do so. The greatest advantage of financial security is the peace of mind that comes from knowing that, whatever challenges life brings, you are equipped to deal with them. You will be better at whatever you choose to do because you can focus on opportunities instead of struggling to eke out a living.

27. IF YOU HAVE NO MAJOR PURPOSE, YOU ARE DRIFTING TOWARD CERTAIN FAILURE.

In achieving the goals you have set for yourself, there are only two alternatives: Either you are moving toward your goal, or you are drifting away from it. Choose your purpose in life and attack it with a vengeance. When you have the courage of your convictions, when the choice is one you've made for yourself, you will have the strength to persevere until you succeed.

28. YOU WILL NEVER BE GREATER THAN THE THOUGHTS THAT DOMINATE YOUR MIND.

If it's true that you become what you think about most, it follows that the quantity and quality of success you achieve in your life will be in direct proportion to the size of your thoughts. If you allow your mind to be dominated by trivial matters, your achievements are likely to be unimportant. Discipline yourself to think about important things. Keep up with what's new in your field and with what's going on in the world. Make a list of good ideas that you can use anytime you are searching for a creative solution to a problem. Remember, small minds think about things; great minds think about ideas.

29. YOUR PROGRESS IN LIFE BEGINS IN YOUR OWN MIND AND ENDS IN THE SAME PLACE.

Every great accomplishment began with the germ of an idea in the mind of a great person, then was shaped for practical usefulness and finally transformed into reality. Make your mind a fertile ground for ideas through constant study and learning, and condition yourself through constant practice to discipline yourself to follow through on your good ideas. The most brilliant concept in the world is only a dream unless you take action. Even a mediocre idea that is put into practice is far more valuable than a flash of genius that languishes in a fallow, undisciplined mind.

30. CONSTANCY OF PURPOSE IS THE FIRST PRINCIPLE OF SUCCESS.

It is critical to your success that you have a well-thought-out plan for your life and that you stick with it regardless of what others may say and the obstacles you encounter. There will always be faultfinders and those who attempt to persuade you that your goals aren't worth the effort you put into achieving them. Those people will never go far, and they will be the first to ask for your help after you have passed them by. Virtually every successful person has considered giving up at some point in his or her struggle to reach the top. And many breakthroughs occurred soon after those same people rededicated themselves to their purpose. There is no known obstacle that cannot be overcome by a person who has constancy of purpose, a Positive Mental Attitude, and the discipline and willpower to succeed.

MAY

Action!

1. IF YOU ARE REALLY GREAT, YOU WILL LET OTHERS DISCOVER THIS FACT FROM YOUR ACTIONS.

In the final analysis, all that really matters are your actions. You may talk a good story, but no matter how good you are at selling others on your capabilities, eventually you have to perform. It is true that people are generally forgiving and will overlook an occasional failure to deliver upon your promises. Ultimately, though, you must live up to your promises to others if you ever expect to make a lasting impression on them.

Make it a habit to demonstrate your abilities before talking about them. Seldom is anything worthwhile achieved without the help of others, and nothing is ever achieved without some form of action. The road to failure and despair is littered with the dreams of those who failed to act upon them.

2. COUNT THAT DAY LOST WHOSE DESCENDING SUN FINDS YOU WITH NO GOOD DEEDS DONE.

It is well known among those who make it a practice to help others that doing a service for another benefits the giver as much as—if not more than—the receiver. When you do a good deed for someone else, you become a better person. The positive effect that your good deed has upon *you* will endure long after it is forgotten by the recipient. Good deeds need not be large or costly. The greatest gifts are gifts of your time and yourself. A kind word or small courtesy will be remembered and appreciated.

3. MEDALS AND TITLES WILL NOT COUNT WHEN YOU GET TO HEAVEN, BUT YOU MAY BE LOOKED OVER CAREFULLY FOR THE SORT OF DEEDS YOU HAVE DONE.

It is a fundamental principle of Christianity, and many other religions, that in the afterlife the only real measure of success will be how you have lived your life, not how much money you have accumulated. Whatever your faith may be, a good rule of everyday behavior is to live your life so that when it is over you can take pride in the knowledge that you have made a difference in the lives of those who have known you.

It's easy in the crush of everyday life to lose sight of the true riches of life, the things that really matter. Psychologist Ilona Tobin defines true success as "giving and receiving love, having physical and mental health, enough wealth to provide you with options, and the time to enjoy them all." Whatever your personal definition of success may be, make sure that it includes a healthy measure of the truly important things in life.

4. THE ONLY SAFE WAY TO BOAST IS BY CONSTRUCTIVE ACTIONS.

It has been said that it's not boasting if you can really do it. This may be true, but a far more persuasive argument is made when you do it first and talk about it later. Besides, good things that are said about you always carry more weight when they are said by someone other than yourself. When you find yourself tempted to wax eloquent about your achievements, force yourself to pause for a moment, take a deep breath, and ask someone else about *their* achievements.

5. WHEN YOU HAVE TALKED YOURSELF INTO WHAT YOU WANT, STOP TALKING AND BEGIN SAYING IT WITH YOUR ACTIONS.

Persuading yourself that you can do something is a strong beginning. Next develop a sound plan and get into action. The longer you delay, the harder it will be to begin.

Seldom is a plan perfect. If you have a clear vision of your goal and a plan that is flexible enough to allow you to deal with unexpected obstacles or take advantage of unforeseen opportunities, don't delay another minute. Just getting into action—even if you do have to make adjustments later—will help focus your mind and channel your energies in the direction of your objective.

6. ACTIONS, NOT WORDS, ARE THE GREATEST MEANS OF SELF-PRAISE.

There are times when you will be asked to put yourself forward, to compete for a position or a contract, and you will have to speak about your accomplishments. Naturally, you will want to put the best foot forward. Be certain, however, that when you do so, you are confident that honest inquiry will support what you say about yourself.

If your actions have been wise and responsible, the record will show this. Leaders in any organization are those who say, "Let's get going. Let's do something rather than wait around to see what happens." When your past actions demonstrate that you are a person who accepts responsibility and shows others the way, your career and relationships will benefit you accordingly.

7. THE VALUE OF ACTIONS DEPENDS ON THE COURAGE THEY REQUIRE.

Ordinary people who do extraordinary things for others are those we later call heroes. When asked why they performed as they did, they often say, "It was nothing anyone else wouldn't have done in the circumstances." Perhaps that's their way of saying we all have the capacity for greatness. It is only when we are severely tested that we rise to the occasion and perform at the highest levels of our competence.

You become a person who does the right thing when presented with great opportunities the same way you achieve success at anything: through force of habit. If you make it a practice to take the appropriate action even when it seems unimportant and insignificant, you will do the right thing—without thinking—in important situations. If you let your actions speak for you, you will never have to worry about others recognizing your contribution.

8. IF YOU REALLY ARE SMARTER THAN OTHERS, SHOW THEM WITH YOUR ACTIONS.

It is a natural human reaction for you to wish to correct others when you see them making a mistake or doing something differently than you would have done it. It is far more difficult to control the impulse to show them how much more intelligent you are. The ability to recognize and control such impulses marks the beginning of the development of wisdom. A wise person knows that when he shows his intelligence with the actions he takes, others learn a far more valuable and lasting lesson.

If you see someone who could benefit from your advice, you can gently lead him to a more appropriate conclusion by asking open-ended, nonjudgmental questions. Let others find the flaws in their reasoning by leading them logically through the process. As Ralph Waldo Emerson once said, "The secret of education lies in respecting the pupil."

9. THE SAFEST AND BEST WAY TO PUNISH ONE WHO HAS DONE YOU AN INJUSTICE IS TO DO HIM OR HER A KIND DEED IN RETURN.

People will always respond in kind, even in greater measure than that which is delivered to them. This commonplace need for retaliation can be replaced with a response designed to convert an enemy into a friend. If you get rid of the millstone of pride, you can respond to an injustice with a kind deed. It may take time to make this work, but if you treat those who dislike you with unfailing kindness, they will eventually succumb to your influence and "retaliate" in kind. As Napoleon Hill said, "The hottest coals of fire ever heaped upon the head of one who has wronged you are the coals of human kindness."

10. WASTE NO WORDS ON A MAN WHO DISLIKES YOU. ACTIONS WILL IMPRESS HIM MORE.

Some people think they can talk their way out of any situation, and for a time they may be right. But if someone already dislikes you, either because of a simple misunderstanding or an error in judgment on your part, he or she will be especially difficult to persuade with words. Their emotions will always get in the way of their ability to think logically and reasonably. Consistent actions over a sustained period of time, however, will usually persuade even the most devout skeptic. If you constantly demonstrate that you are a generous, kind, and caring person, it will be very hard for even your enemies to dislike you. In any case, you will become a better person for having made the effort.

11. BY ALL MEANS TELL THE WORLD HOW GOOD YOU ARE—BUT . . .

You should let others know of your achievements, with these provisions: Do it with your actions first and make sure you share the credit with others who helped you along the way. A fundamental principle of leadership that has not changed over the centuries is: Share the credit for success with others, but take the blame for failures alone.

12. IF YOU THINK YOU CAN BUY YOUR WAY INTO HEAVEN WITH MONEY ALONE, YOU MAY REGRET THAT YOU DIDN'T CONVERT IT INTO GOOD DEEDS INSTEAD.

If through some terrible, unforeseen tragedy you should die tomorrow, how would your epitaph read? What would others remember about you? In the final analysis, you will be remembered for your good works, not for the money you have accumulated during your lifetime. Your wealth may be little more than the cause for disagreements among your heirs, while your good deeds will be remembered long after you are gone. As you accumulate wealth, devote a portion of your money and your time to causes that benefit those less fortunate than you.

13. OFFER RESULTS, NOT ALIBIS.

There are many people who—perhaps with the best of intentions—make promises they somehow never get around to keeping. These folks have usually developed a number of perfectly plausible explanations for not meeting their commitments; they have become experts at explaining away their failures. Successful people, though, are those who accept responsibility for their lives. They know that talk is cheap; actions are all that really matter.

The world is waiting for men and women who seek the opportunity to render *real service*—the kind of service that lightens the burdens of their neighbors, the kind of service that 95 percent of people *do not render* because they do not understand it. When you provide a truly useful service, enthusiastically and in a spirit of genuine helpfulness, success will automatically follow. The world seeks out such individuals and rewards them accordingly.

14. IT'S NOT THE EPITAPH ON YOUR TOMBSTONE BUT THE RECORD OF YOUR DEEDS THAT MAY PERPETUATE YOUR NAME AFTER DEATH.

Alfred Nobel had an opportunity afforded to very few. When his brother died, the newspaper confused the two and published Alfred's obituary instead of his brother's. As he read his own obituary, Alfred realized that the world would remember him for his invention of dynamite—an instrument of destruction. It was because of that experience that he decided to fund the Nobel Prizes. Today, most of the world knows his name in connection with humankind's greatest achievements.

Good deeds live on in the minds of others. When you do a kindness for someone else, you set in motion a force for good that will remain long after you're gone.

15. THE WORLD PINS NO MEDALS ON YOU BECAUSE OF WHAT YOU KNOW, BUT IT MAY CROWN YOU WITH GLORY AND RICHES FOR WHAT YOU DO.

Knowledge is an important component of success in any field. To accomplish anything worthwhile often requires years of study. But knowledge alone is not power; it becomes powerful only when it is applied through positive action.

Study after study of successful people reveals that they

have a bias for action. They gather the appropriate facts, relate them to their knowledge about the subject, develop an implementation plan, and then get into action. When in doubt, it's far better to act too soon rather than too late.

16. FAITH IS A COMBINATION OF THOUGHTS AND ACTIONS.

When you apply your faith in yourself, your faith in your fellow man, and your faith in God, the result is a positive course of action that when persistently followed will almost always lead to success. When you believe in your ideas and in your abilities, and you trust in the Infinite Intelligence of the universe, you know that your thoughts and deeds will ultimately lead to a successful conclusion. You cannot fail.

17. IF YOU APPRECIATE THE KINDNESS SHOWN YOU BY OTHERS, SAY IT WITH ACTIONS AS WELL AS WORDS.

The people who enjoy the greatest financial and personal success in life are those who build lasting relationships—with business associates, friends, co-workers, and others. They take the time and trouble to stay in touch, and they make sure that when someone does a good deed for them, they respond in kind. Build your network of personal and professional friends by taking the initiative and *being* a friend.

18. EVERYTHING YOU CREATE OR ACQUIRE BEGINS IN THE FORM OF DESIRE.

In order to act, you must have a purpose. If you want to act successfully in all but the most mundane affairs, you must embrace that purpose with a burning desire. Many people *think* they want to be successful, but since they do not back that thought with an intense drive, they never achieve success.

Cultivate your desire. Feed it with thoughts of yourself enjoying whatever it is you seek. It's like stoking the furnace of a steam engine. You need to build up enough pressure to carry yourself over hills; if your desire doesn't burn hotly enough, you'll find yourself stalled and rolling backwards. The secret to action is a red-hot desire.

19. THE RIGHT SORT OF ACTIONS REQUIRE NO EMBELLISHMENT OF WORDS.

One of the most common mistakes is making excuses to explain why we do not succeed. Unfortunately, the vast majority of people in the world—those who do not succeed—are excuse-makers. They try to explain their action, or inaction, with words. When you succeed, accept the congratulations of others with good grace; when you fail, take responsibility for your actions, learn from your mistakes, and move on to more constructive things. When your actions are appropriate in every circumstance, you will never feel the need to explain them with words. Your actions will say all that needs to be said.

20. WATCH THE ONE AHEAD OF YOU, AND YOU'LL LEARN WHY HE IS AHEAD. THEN EMULATE HIM.

One of the surest ways to achieve success is to observe the actions of successful people, determine what principles they regularly employ, and then use them yourself. The principles of success, as Andrew Carnegie said, are definite, they are real, and they can be learned by anyone willing to take the time to study and apply them. If you are truly observant, you will find that you can learn something from almost everyone you meet. And it isn't even necessary that you know them. You may choose great people who are no longer alive. The important thing is to study their lives, and then learn and apply in your own life the specific principles these people used to achieve greatness.

21. IF YOU WANT A JOB DONE PROMPTLY AND WELL, GET A BUSY PERSON TO DO IT. THE IDLE ONE KNOWS TOO MANY SUBSTITUTES AND SHORTCUTS.

Most of us will never know our true capacity for achievement because we never challenge ourselves to perform at our best every day. This truism becomes apparent when you are presented with an opportunity that really interests you. No matter how busy you may be, somehow you will find the time to pursue it. Conversely, duties that have little appeal for you are easily postponed and eventually forgotten.

Busy people are not procrastinators. They know that life, as John David Wright once observed about business, "is like riding a bicycle. Either you keep moving, or you fall down." The most effective people have a sense of urgency. They set deadlines and force themselves to establish priorities. Even if your activities don't usually require strict deadlines, set them for yourself. You will be amazed at how much you can accomplish in a short time—if that's all the time you have.

22. THE MAN WHO DOESN'T REACH DECISIONS PROMPTLY WHEN HE HAS ALL NECESSARY FACTS IN HAND CANNOT BE DEPENDED ON TO CARRY OUT DECISIONS AFTER HE MAKES THEM.

There is no one right answer—but an endless number of right answers—to most of life's problems. Usually, your options are many and varied; the difficulty lies in choosing the best alternative from among many, all in a reasonable time frame. If you devote yourself to making small decisions promptly, you will find it much easier to be decisive when the stakes are much bigger. Most important, you'll find making decisions and acting on them far easier if you act promptly.

23. THE INDIVIDUAL WHO ONLY DOES ENOUGH WORK TO GET BY SELDOM GETS MUCH MORE THAN "BY."

There is a cause-and-effect relationship between your actions and the rewards that accrue to you. When you put more of yourself into your career, your personal relationships, your religious faith, and any other aspect of your life, you get more out of it. If your ambitions are greater than simply "getting by" in life, you will never be truly happy with your company, your job, or yourself unless you do your best every day. Your harshest critic and your toughest competitor should be you.

24. GOOD INTENTIONS ARE USELESS UNTIL THEY ARE EXPRESSED IN APPROPRIATE ACTION.

Good intentions may be an appropriate starting point for achievement, but they will go nowhere unless you follow through with action. Many people confuse intentions with achievement; after all, it is the idea that is most important, they reason. In reality, the most mediocre idea acted upon is far more valuable than a flash of genius that resides only in your mind. Developing the habit of action may be difficult at first, but the more you practice it, the easier it becomes.

25. IT TAKES MORE THAN A NAME ON A CHURCH MEMBERSHIP TO MAKE A CHRISTIAN.

Christianity is not a passive religion; it is the active application of your beliefs. Simply understanding the basic tenets of faith is not enough. Being a Christian means actively practicing your religion, taking positive actions to improve your character, and behaving kindly and generously toward others. The Bible is filled with instructions for living a good and decent life, and all involve constructive action on the part of believers.

In any aspect of your life, you may choose to be an observer or an active participant. You may learn a great deal from observation, but there comes a time when you will be measured by your own contribution, not simply what you've learned by watching others. The principle is the same in your religious, personal, or business life. In the final analysis, you will be measured not by the depth of your beliefs, but by the actions you take because of them.

26. REMEMBER, A KITE FLIES AGAINST THE WIND, NOT WITH IT.

It is important to recognize from the beginning that success will not be achieved easily. Achievers—like a kite struggling against the gusts—soar to great heights, firmly anchored to a philosophy of success that keeps them on course, regardless of the difficulties they encounter along the way.

Make sure you are anchored to a philosophy that will sustain you despite the difficulties you will most certainly face in your quest for success. When you know what you are about, when you have definite goals and a plan for achieving them, you may be buffeted by the winds of circumstance, but you will never be blown permanently off course. The stronger the wind, the higher you will fly.

27. THE BEST POSSIBLE WAY TO GET A TRANSFER FROM THE JOB YOU DON'T LIKE TO ONE YOU LIKE BETTER IS TO DO YOUR PRESENT JOB SO WELL THE MANAGEMENT WILL DESIRE TO USE YOUR SKILL ON A MORE IMPORTANT JOB.

You will achieve far more in your life if you make it a practice to perform first the tasks you like the least. When you are known as a conscientious worker who welcomes difficult assignments, it is inevitable that you will be given more and more responsibility in the organization. And by doing the hardest jobs first you can take advantage of your higher energy level at the beginning of the day. You can then coast through the more routine tasks. Also, with important work done early, you can better deal with unexpected interruptions during the day.

28. NEVER MIND WHAT OTHERS DIDN'T DO. IT'S WHAT YOU DO THAT COUNTS.

If you depend upon others for your success, you are doomed to a life of failure and despair. It is a sad fact of life that few people consistently deliver what they promise. Instead of lamenting what someone else should have done to help you, focus on what you can do to help yourself. The best plan of action is one that provides opportunities for others to benefit if they wish to work with you toward the accomplishment of your goals but that does not depend upon these people for success.

29. LIFE SAYS, "MAKE GOOD OR MAKE ROOM, BUT DON'T MAKE EXCUSES."

In today's management parlance, "Lead, follow, or get out of the way." When you are actively working toward a goal, there are no failures; there are only degrees of success.

Choose to be a leader. Take the initiative. When you are faced with a problem or a difficult decision, don't waste endless hours agonizing over the solution. If you analyze the situation objectively, you will always find an answer. Don't focus on the problem; focus on the solution. Then get into action. As W. Clement Stone has often said, "The emotions are not always subject to reason, but they are always subject to *action!*"

30. THE WORLD STANDS ASIDE AND MAKES ROOM FOR THE PERSON WHO KNOWS WHERE HE IS GOING AND IS ON HIS WAY.

When you have a vision for what you wish to achieve in your life, not only will others stand aside and let you pass, but they will join you in your quest as well. They will instinctively recognize your enthusiasm and zest for living. When you speak of your passion in life, your definite major goal, they will see the intensity of your desire, and they will respond with encouragement and assistance or they will stand aside. It will be apparent to all who know you that you *will* succeed.

31. IT'S A SURE THING THAT YOU'LL NOT FINISH IF YOU DON'T START.

An ancient proverb says, "The journey of a thousand miles begins with a single step." You have probably known people nearing the end of their life's journey who looked back and said, "If only I had done things differently. . . . If only I had taken advantage of that opportunity when it came along." Unfulfilled lives are filled with "if only"s. They are the refrain of the timid souls whose lives were finished before they ever really got started.

Life is filled with many opportunities—for great successes and spectacular failures. It is up to you to seize the initiative, to take advantage of the opportunities that come your way. You are condemned to a life of mediocrity—unless you get into *action*. Don't delay; do it today!

JUNE

Opportunity

1. OPPORTUNITY HAS A QUEER WAY OF STALKING THE PERSON WHO CAN RECOGNIZE IT AND IS READY TO EMBRACE IT.

It is a curious quirk of human nature that some people can see opportunities, while others only see problems. When you train your mind to seek out opportunities, you will find that every day literally presents you with more opportunities than you can take advantage of. They will be all around you. Instead of your seeking opportunities, they will seek *you* out. Your biggest problem will be choosing the best ones.

The first step in making sure you are ready to recognize opportunities when they occur is to make sure you have a clear understanding of your own core competencies. Realistically assess your strengths and weaknesses as though you were reviewing the credentials of a total stranger. Identify what areas you're best in and those where you need improvement. Work on your weaknesses and build upon your strengths so that when you recognize opportunities you are prepared to capitalize upon them.

2. THOSE WHO ARE QUICK TO SEE THEIR LIMITATIONS GENERALLY ARE SLOW IN SEEING THEIR OPPORTUNITIES.

Movie producer Michael Todd once said, "Being broke is temporary; being poor is a state of mind." So it is with opportunity. Whether you see opportunities or limitations is entirely within your control. How you view the world is a reflection of your mental attitude. If you focus on your inadequacies, you will be plagued by fear, doubt, and failure, but when you focus on your strengths, you will find courage, confidence, and success.

Self-confidence can replace self-doubt only by deliberate, planned effort. When you start to doubt your capabilities, pause to review your previous accomplishments. Identify every experience that might be helpful to you in your present situation. When you apply the knowledge and wisdom you have accumulated, there are few limitations that you cannot overcome.

3. DON'T EVER ADMIT THAT THE WORLD HAS NOT GIVEN YOU AN OPPORTUNITY.

Opportunities are never just handed to you; they must be created. Opportunities abound for every individual in every walk of life. They may not be the opportunities that you prefer, but each opportunity of which you take advantage leads to bigger and better opportunities. Physical and mental handicaps may mean that you have to explore territories unknown to others, but they also mean you have opportunities those others will never find. Think of Stephen Hawking's brilliant research on the nature of the universe despite the fact that a crippling disease makes writing and speaking, as we know it, impossible for him.

Those who approach their jobs and careers with enthusiasm always find plenty of opportunities, while those who complain about no one ever giving them a chance are merely observers of life. When you are determined that you will not allow others to determine your future for you, when you refuse to allow temporary setbacks to defeat you, you are destined for great success. The opportunities will always be there for you.

4. IF IT ISN'T YOUR JOB TO DO IT, PERHAPS IT IS YOUR OPPORTUNITY.

Someone once observed that the reason we often fail to recognize opportunities is because they come disguised as problems. When a customer, a colleague, or your boss has a problem, it may create a valuable opportunity for you. It isn't important to the person with the problem how your company is organized or whose responsibility it is to solve the problem; he or she only wants the situation resolved.

The next time a customer, a colleague, or your boss asks for your assistance in something that falls outside your area of responsibility, instead of referring them to someone else, offer to help. Look at the situation from the other person's point of view. How would you like the situation handled if the roles were reversed? Take the initiative to find the answer, solve the problem, or keep the project moving forward.

5. OPPORTUNITY OFTEN KNOCKS—ONLY TO FIND NO ONE IN.

The world is filled with unfortunate souls who didn't hear opportunity's knock at the door because they were down at the convenience store buying lottery tickets. They have never learned that, as Branch Rickey, general manager of the Brooklyn Dodgers from 1942–50, once observed, "Luck is the residue of design." You will be surprised how much your luck will improve when you make sure you are prepared to take advantage of opportunities.

How many times have you had a great idea that you failed to act upon, only to discover later that someone used the same idea to start a business, get a promotion, or find a better job? Resolve now to get into action when you have a good idea. Don't wait for something to happen—make it happen!

6. A RESOURCEFUL PERSON WILL ALWAYS MAKE OPPORTUNITY FIT HIS OR HER NEEDS.

The ability to recognize opportunities is a critical element of success, but it is only the beginning. An idea is valuable only if it can be put into practice—by you. Highly successful people know that there are many ways to capitalize on an opportunity. They evaluate and shape it to fit their capabilities, or they put together a team composed of people with the skills necessary to take advantage of it—whatever it takes to make it work. Seldom is there any single right answer in business. Often there are any number of right answers.

7. OPPORTUNITY WASTES NO EFFORT LOOKING FOR THE PERSON WHO IS WASTING TIME THROUGH IDLENESS OR DESTRUCTIVE ACTION.

Opportunities somehow always seem to gravitate toward busy people who can hardly keep up with those they already have. Logically, it would seem that opportunities would make an effort to seek out individuals who have an abundance of time available, but instead opportunities appear for those who have goals and dreams and a plan for achieving them. We often think of opportunity as a living, moving thing, something that actively seeks out a willing recipient. In fact, the reverse is true. Opportunities are ideas or concepts that exist only in the minds of those who recognize them. When you have no goals or plans, opportunities mean nothing to you. They become opportunities only when you recognize them as ideas that you can implement to help you move toward your goal.

8. OPPORTUNITY WILL NOT INTEREST ITSELF IN THE PERSON WHO ISN'T INTERESTED IN IT.

In a free and democratic society, the number of opportunities for achievement is virtually limitless. In every business or profession, there are innumerable opportunities to invent new products, to improve manufacturing and administrative processes, and to offer better service than the competitor down the street. But every opportunity will soon drift away unless someone seizes it and puts it to work.

Anytime you are faced with a difficult problem, stop for a moment and ask yourself: "What is the opportunity hidden in this problem?" When you find an opportunity, you will be far ahead of your competitors.

9. THOSE WHO WILL NOT TAKE A CHANCE SELDOM HAVE ONE THRUST UPON THEM.

Success always involves risk. You must take a chance by investing your time, money, and effort. It pays to be thoughtful and deliberate in your analyses of opportunities, but don't let timidity hold you back.

Because you have worked hard to develop those things you must risk, it is natural for you to place a high value on them. But what use are they if you do not put them to use? You will recognize opportunity only to the extent that you are willing to consider risking your time, money, and effort. Being confident gives you the courage to face risk and act when opportunity arises. No one on earth is going to force success upon you; you will find it only to the degree that you actively seek it out.

10. OPPORTUNITY LETS YOU PUT YOUR FOOT INSIDE THE DOOR OF SUCCESS, BUT IT DOESN'T BREAK THE DOOR DOWN FOR YOU.

Opportunities are not windfalls. Winning a sweepstakes makes you instantly rich; encountering an opportunity means you will have to go to work. When you have attuned your mind to recognize opportunities, you will understand that most often they involve the exploitation of some potential, such as providing a new or better service, streamlining production, or reaching a new market.

This is why the habit of initiative is so important. You must be prepared to act as soon as you recognize an opportunity. The action may be simply further investigation, or it may be making an instant sale. Most often, however, an opportunity takes time and perseverance to develop.

11. OPPORTUNITY NEVER SNEAKS UP ON THOSE WHO STRADDLE THE FENCE OF INDECISION.

Successful people are decisive people. When opportunities come their way, they evaluate them carefully, make a decision, and take appropriate action. They know that indecision wastes time that could be spent on more productive tasks. They also avoid unnecessary risks by implementing their decisions gradually. They don't attempt to make every decision at the beginning. Each action is contingent upon the success of the one that preceded it.

Benjamin Franklin, one of America's wisest men, is said to have used a simple method to make difficult decisions. He drew a line down the center of a sheet of paper, and on one side he listed the "pros" of the decision; on the other, he listed the "cons." In addition to simplifying the decision-making process, the list also served as a graphic illustration of the advantages and disadvantages of any decision, regardless of its complexity. The impact of the decision could then be quickly and easily assessed.

12. ARE YOU WAITING FOR SUCCESS TO ARRIVE, OR ARE YOU GOING OUT TO FIND WHERE IT IS HIDING?

If you are waiting for success to seek you out, you are headed for a big disappointment. Success is rarely forced upon anyone, and it will never overtake you unexpectedly. You must prepare for it and actively seek it out if you ever plan to achieve any measure of success in your life. Constantly be alert to changes in your business or profession. Subscribe to trade magazines and professional journals, join industry associations or professional societies, and get to know the experts in the field in order to keep abreast of new developments.

13. THERE ISN'T MUCH ONE CAN DO FOR THE INDIVIDUAL WHO WILL NOT TRY TO DO SOMETHING FOR HIMSELF.

One of the keys to success is Personal Initiative. Most people —including those who will play a key role in the level of success you achieve in your life—will not give you their full assistance and support unless you first take the initiative. If you see something that needs to be done, just do it. Wendy's founder, Dave Thomas, says, "A little initiative will improve your luck nine days out of ten."

14. A LITTLE JOB WELL DONE IS THE FIRST STEP TOWARD A BIGGER ONE.

Success is more of a process than an event. Great success is achieved after a long string of small successes. Most of us earn our stripes one step at a time, and we work our way up through the ranks. When we begin our careers, we are given assignments that are commensurate with our skill and experience. As we prove our worth to the organization, we are gradually entrusted with more responsibility and increasingly larger projects. As you assume responsibility for one position, do so with an eye toward the next one. Do your absolute best every day in your job, but always plan for the future. View each day as an opportunity to learn something that will make you more valuable to the company or organization so that when the time arrives for promotions, your name will be the first one that comes to your boss's mind.

15. DON'T ASK YOUR EMPLOYER WHY YOU ARE NOT PROMOTED. ASK THE PERSON WHO REALLY KNOWS BEST—YOURSELF.

There is only one person who is in charge of your career progression, and that person is you. Lee Iacocca is said to have written his entire career plan on the back of a business card. On it were the promotions he expected to earn and the dates he expected to receive them—until he was named CEO of the company. Successful people know that they must create their own opportunities and be ready for them when they arrive.

Some organizations have clearly defined career paths while others are more informal in their approach, but if you study the senior people in the company, you can quickly identify the kind of education and experience you need to advance. If you are with the right company, one that excites and enthuses you, identify the career moves you'd like to make and get to work making yourself qualified for the job you want.

16. JUST WHAT ARE YOU WAITING FOR AND WHY ARE YOU WAITING?

Far too many people spend their entire lives waiting for that glorious day when the perfect opportunity presents itself to them. Too late, they realize that each day held opportunity for those who sought it out.

If you have not formulated a plan for what you would like to accomplish in your life, don't waste another minute. When you have Definiteness of Purpose fueled by a burning desire to reach your objectives, nothing can stand in your way. Don't wait around waiting for life to happen to you. When you know what you want and how you expect to earn it, life will agree to your terms, not the other way around.

17. LIVE EACH DAY AS IF IT WERE YOUR LAST, AND YOU'LL DEVELOP A KEEN RESPECT FOR OPPORTUNITY.

If you had only one more day on this earth, how much sharper your senses would be. The beauty of nature, the simple pleasures of life, would be indescribably wonderful, and every moment would present an opportunity to spend quality time with your family and strengthen relationships with friends, acquaintances, and business associates. Every thought would be laser-sharp in that highly focused state. Well, today *is* the last day on earth for *today's* opportunities. Don't let them pass you by.

18. MOST MISFORTUNES ARE THE RESULT OF MISUSED TIME.

The only luck in the world is the luck you create for yourself. Only in the casino are the odds in favor of the house. In real life, the odds always favor those who use their time wisely to pursue their goals constructively, to fill every day with a full measure of honest work. Bad luck befalls those who waste time and mental energy hoping for the big break that will propel them to greatness. We all have the same twenty-four hours available to us in each day. Most of us spend eight hours working and eight hours sleeping. What you do with the remaining eight hours will have a tremendous influence on the level of success you achieve in your life.

19. THE MOST INTERESTING THING ABOUT A POSTAGE STAMP IS THE PERSISTENCE WITH WHICH IT STICKS TO ITS JOB.

The tiny, insignificant postage stamp is a good example of what it is possible to achieve if you stick with the job until it is finished. Inconspicuously stuck on the corner of the envelope, it provides the impetus to keep moving until the entire packet reaches its ultimate destination. The influence you may have upon your company, your church, your family, or any organization is incalculable if you have the persistence to pursue your goal until you achieve it. It is an absolute certainty that you will encounter obstacles in any worthwhile endeavor. When you do, remember the inconsequential little postage stamp and stick with the job until it is finished.

20. ANYONE CAN QUIT WHEN THE GOING IS HARD, BUT A THOROUGHBRED NEVER QUITS UNTIL HE WINS.

The going is always hard on the road to greatness. If success were easy, everyone would achieve it. NFL All-Pro lineman Brian Holloway recalled that when he was playing for the New England Patriots and the Los Angeles Raiders, there wasn't a single day when he didn't feel like giving up because the road was too tough and the sacrifices were too great. He didn't quit, of course; he was willing to pay the price because he was determined to succeed. True Thoroughbreds never quit. Competition only spurs them, and obstacles merely reinforce their determination to succeed. If you have not yet achieved greatness in your life, it is because you have been willing to settle for less. You may not cross the finish line first every time you try, but if you stay in the race, you will eventually prevail.

21. VICTORY IS ALWAYS POSSIBLE FOR THE PERSON WHO REFUSES TO STOP FIGHTING.

Julius Caesar had long wished to capture the British. He sailed to the British Isles, quietly unloaded his troops and supplies, and gave the order to burn the ships. He then called all of his men together and said, "Now it is win or perish. We have no choice." With that single order, he guaranteed the success of his campaign. He knew that people who have no other alternative—or will accept no other—always win.

If you find yourself in a situation where victory seems impossible, you may benefit your cause by developing an alternate course of action. If your objective won't yield to a full frontal assault, try an oblique approach. There are very few problems in life that are impossible to solve, and few obstacles that will not eventually give way to a determined, motivated person with a plan that is flexible enough to cope with changing conditions.

22. NATURE YIELDS HER MOST PROFOUND SECRETS TO THOSE WHO ARE DETERMINED TO UNCOVER THEM.

The field of science is perhaps the best illustration of how success always seems to come to those who apply the principle of accurate thinking in a persistent, determined effort. America's great inventor Thomas A. Edison is said to have failed 10,000 times in his attempt to develop a workable electric lightbulb. He learned from each failure and refused to quit until he succeeded. Breakthroughs occur every day because a determined person continues to search for solutions to complex problems long after everyone else has given up and gone home. You may not invent the lightbulb or the next supercomputer, but you can find creative solutions to old problems if you apply the proven principles of success consistently and persistently.

23. BEFORE WORRYING ABOUT HOW TO GET MORE PAY, TRY THINKING HOW YOU CAN DO A BETTER JOB AND YOU MAY NOT NEED TO WORRY.

When you devote your time and efforts to doing your best at every job you do, instead of developing persuasive arguments why you should be paid more for what you do, the pay raises will take care of themselves. When you approach every job enthusiastically in a spirit of friendly cooperation, you distinguish yourself from the vast majority of people whose primary concerns include breaks, benefits, paychecks, and quitting time. Don't complain about your status or your pay to anyone, not even to your best friend. Word will eventually get back to the boss. Which type of worker would you rather have on your team: one who complains constantly or one who is always helpful, cheerful, and reliable?

24. HENRY FORD IS REPORTED TO HAVE OFFERED $25,000 TO ANYONE WHO WOULD SHOW HIM HOW TO SAVE A SINGLE NUT AND BOLT ON EACH AUTOMOBILE HE MADE.

Without Henry Ford, our country would not be the America we know today. His obsession with reducing costs and improving productivity allowed him to build the first automobile that ordinary people could afford and led to the construction of a vast network of roads and highways that gave birth to today's mobile society. It also set the stage for total quality management and continuous improvement programs that are prevalent in the automotive industry today.

We would all be well advised to take a page from the lessons that the automotive industry has learned in recent years. An obsessive focus on the needs and wants of our customers allows us to become an indispensable part of their lives, but nothing is forever. Continuous improvement is expected in virtually every industry, and quality is the minimum requirement in today's global economy. Leaders are those who significantly outperform the competition in every aspect of the business.

25. SHOW ME HOW TO SAVE A THIN DIME ON ANY OPERATION IN THE PLANT, AND I'LL SHOW YOU HOW TO GET QUICK AND ADEQUATE PROMOTION.

When you search for ways to save money for your company, you are thinking like a manager or owner. Every manager worth his paycheck knows that in a high-volume manufacturing operation a savings of a few pennies on any process will quickly add up to thousands of dollars. And an individual who figures out a way to save the company thousands of dollars is marked for advancement; he or she is simply too valuable not to promote.

The best person to improve productivity in your job is you. No other person knows your job as intimately as you do. Motivate yourself to improve continually by competing with yourself. As you perform a specific task, look for shortcuts that will help you finish it faster. Use the time you save to analyze other parts of your job, volunteer to help others with difficult or time-consuming tasks, or to tackle a new, more rewarding assignment.

26. MANY SUCCESSFUL PEOPLE HAVE FOUND OPPORTUNITIES IN FAILURE AND ADVERSITY THAT THEY COULD NOT RECOGNIZE IN MORE FAVORABLE CIRCUMSTANCES.

Samuel Johnson once observed that the prospect of being hanged wonderfully focuses the mind. You yourself may have found that your mind seems sharpest when you are faced with the greatest difficulties. Desperation often proves you really are better than you think. But with the exception of an immediate threat to your life or health, there are few situations that require instantaneous action. When the world seems to be conspiring against you and nothing is working out right, pause for a few moments to think the situation through—then develop the most appropriate plan of action, the one that has the greatest likelihood of success.

27. DON'T OVERLOOK SMALL DETAILS. REMEMBER THAT THE UNIVERSE AND ALL THAT IS IN IT ARE MADE FROM TINY ATOMS.

There is an old expression that says, "If you take care of the little things, the big things will take care of themselves." It's another way of saying that every job is composed of many small details, any one of which, if overlooked, can create big problems later. If you have trouble dealing with details— paperwork, expense accounts, and other annoying details— set aside a time during your work cycle (daily, weekly, or monthly) to deal with such unpleasant tasks. Prepare yourself mentally to deal with those tasks, and you may find that you dispense with them quickly and efficiently. You may even find that the job wasn't nearly as unpleasant as you expected it to be.

28. YOUR JOB WILL DO NO MORE FOR YOU THAN YOU DO FOR IT.

Any job contains opportunities for personal growth if you approach it as a positive learning experience. Just as every business is required to adapt to new technologies, new competitors, and countless other changes that routinely occur, so is every individual. If you are not learning and advancing in your job, you are stagnating and falling behind. It is impossible to stand still. View each day as an opportunity to learn something new, to improve yourself, and then do one thing better than you have ever done it before. In a dynamic organization, it is impossible to master every task; just when you think you have everything figured out, things change. Accept such changes as a necessary aspect of business, one that makes life interesting and exciting. You will find your job much more enjoyable when you do, and you will indeed find that it does more for you than you do for it.

29. ABILITY IS GREATER THAN MONEY BECAUSE IT CAN BE NEITHER LOST NOR STOLEN.

If you study the lives of very successful people, you will find that they rarely climb to the top of their business or profession and stay there. They often climb to the top and fall to the bottom several times during their careers, but they know that the one thing that got them where they are—their ability—is always there to help them reach the top again. Your ability is the one thing that you own exclusively; no one can ever take it from you.

30. WHEN YOU CLOSE THE DOOR OF YOUR MIND TO NEGATIVE THOUGHTS, THE DOOR OF OPPORTUNITY OPENS TO YOU.

It is the nature of opportunity that it simply refuses to attach itself to negative thinkers. Negative minds cannot conceive exciting new business opportunities, invent innovative new products, solve difficult problems, or create beautiful music or works of art. All of these activities require a positive belief in yourself and your abilities. When you approach every challenge with a Positive Mental Attitude, you will always discover opportunities that others have overlooked. Relish your achievements and recall them when the going gets tough. Take comfort in the knowledge that you have succeeded in the past and you can do it again. *You can do it if you think you can!*

JULY

The Power of Teamwork

1. UNLESS YOU ARE AN ARMY OFFICER, YOU CAN GET BETTER RESULTS BY REQUESTS THAN YOU CAN BY ORDERS.

Armies spend endless hours training people to follow orders without question. It's an essential quality in a soldier. In everyday life, however, things don't work that way. Business, political, and civic leaders have learned that ordinary people will perform exceptional tasks when they are asked—not ordered—to do so.

Even when you are managing other people, you will achieve far more if you convert every order to a request. Introductory phrases such as, "Would you mind . . ." or "Could I ask your assistance in . . ." or the always effective "Please . . ." will ensure success far more often than intimidating those who work for you. And when you need help from those whose paychecks you do not control, you will find them far more responsive to requests than to orders.

2. NO ONE IS CAPABLE OF GIVING DIRECTION UNLESS HE OR SHE KNOWS HOW TO TAKE DIRECTIONS AND CARRY THEM OUT.

An essential quality of leadership is developing the ability to persuade others to align their goals with yours and those of the organization. Until you, yourself, are able to join forces with others in the pursuit of a common objective, you will never persuade them to join your cause. Effective leaders recognize the value of working together, and they learn how to follow directions before being entrusted with the responsibility for the performance of others.

Good leaders show by example how they expect others to behave. Even though the troops may be trained to follow orders unquestioningly, the officer always leads them into battle. You cannot push others to follow your example; you must pull them along with you. When you show by your every word and deed that you are a person of character, one who works for the greater good of the entire organization, your people will follow.

3. WILLING COOPERATION PRODUCES ENDURING POWER, WHILE FORCED COOPERATION ENDS IN FAILURE.

No civilization based upon the unjust treatment of its people has ever endured. A tyrant may force the cooperation of others for a time, but that power is never sustained. Only when people are accorded the respect they deserve do they willingly create and maintain successful organizations and societies. When you build a company or an organization based on fairness and justice for every member, you have built a power that will long endure.

The best way to secure the commitment and unending cooperation of others is through the simple application of the Golden Rule. It is the most successful and long-lasting management theory ever developed. When you treat others as you would like to be treated were you in their situation, you will inspire loyalty and enthusiastic cooperation. Set high standards for yourself and others, treat them well, let them do their jobs, and they will perform miracles for you.

4. TRY TELLING YOUR BOSS ABOUT THE THINGS YOU LIKE, AND SEE HOW WILLINGLY HE OR SHE WILL HELP YOU GET RID OF THE THINGS YOU DON'T LIKE.

In recent years, great strides have been made in overcoming the traditional adversarial relationship between workers and bosses. At last we're learning that when we focus on better serving our clients and customers, everybody wins. When you begin to focus on what's good in your company instead of what you don't like, you will be amazed how quickly you will have more responsibility, and soon you will be teaching your employees how to do your old job.

5. FRIENDLY COOPERATION WILL GET YOU FAR MORE THAN UNFRIENDLY AGITATION IN ANY MARKET.

When you treat your competitors with the courtesy and respect you would like, most will respond in kind, and the result is a stable, productive, profitable industry. On the other hand, an industry or market that is composed of vicious, unethical competitors will soon destroy itself. When you are asked how your products and services compare with those of your competitors, speak respectfully and politely about your rivals, but use the question to shift the discussion to your company and your products. Acknowledge others' good points, and then move on. If you complain too much about the competition, prospective customers may wonder what they are missing and refuse to buy until they have compared your products and services with those of others.

6. NO ONE CAN SUCCEED AND REMAIN SUCCESSFUL WITHOUT THE FRIENDLY COOPERATION OF OTHERS.

In today's interdependent society, it is virtually impossible in any business, profession, or occupation for an individual to achieve great heights of success without the help of others. The best way to get friendly cooperation is to give it. When you make it a practice to encourage others and to help them advance in their careers whenever possible, most will reciprocate when you need their help. Give generously, and you will benefit in kind.

7. COOPERATION MUST START AT THE HEAD OF A DEPARTMENT IF IT IS EXPECTED AT THE OTHER END. THE SAME IS TRUE FOR EFFICIENCY.

In most large organizations, the amount of time and energy that is squandered in interdepartmental rivalry is enormous. Managers who compete with others inside the company waste valuable resources that should be directed at fulfilling the company's mission to serve its customers better. Worse, a negative, internal focus can cause the company to miss opportunities, the full effect of which may not be realized for months or even years. Whether you are the head of the department or the newest worker on the staff, you can help your company immeasurably by refusing to become embroiled in internal strife. Compete with yourself to do the best job you can do instead of competing with others.

8. FRIENDLY COOPERATION IS NEVER ANY PART OF THE DEVIL'S WORK. HE IS WORKING ON THE OTHER SIDE.

The most noble human relationships are those that have been formed in a spirit of cooperation and harmony. Cooperation, in many ways, is the physical manifestation of your care and concern for your fellow man. When you work with others in a spirit of friendly cooperation, you are conducting yourself according to the founding principles of most religions and all successful societies. Everyone occasionally feels pangs of jealousy or envy, usually accompanied by the urge to cause problems or difficulty for those we dislike. Truly successful people have learned to restrain such urges. They know that if they concentrate upon their own objectives and help others along the way, they will eventually reach their goals. It isn't easy to always be a friendly, cooperative person, but in the end you will find that it is worth the effort.

9. FRIENDLY COOPERATION ALWAYS PAYS OFF BECAUSE THIS SORT OF TEAMWORK CREATES A POSITIVE MENTAL ATTITUDE, WHICH DOES NOT RECOGNIZE OBSTACLES.

In any organized endeavor, obstacles are going to occur. Sometimes they appear in the form of technical problems; sometimes they are disputes between members of the team over which course is best to follow. If you have set an example of initiative and open communication, you will find that your team has the mental and spiritual resources to overcome these kinds of struggles.

A group of people who trust their leader and one another don't waste energy jockeying for prestige. They know that they will all benefit from a solution, and they are motivated to find it by sharing the knowledge and ideas. From these many parts a skilled leader can create the necessary solution, but only if a spirit of friendliness and honesty prevails.

10. THOSE WHO CAN'T TAKE DIRECTIONS GRACIOUSLY HAVE NO BUSINESS GIVING THEM.

If you are an irresponsible or argumentative worker who cannot accept instructions from others, you are destined to remain at the bottom of the workforce. Before you can ever hope to manage other people, you must learn to manage yourself and your relationships with others effectively, particularly with those in higher positions in the organization. Unless you can learn how to manage your relationship with your own boss or bosses, you will never be able to manage a relationship with your subordinates.

11. REMEMBER THAT NO ONE CAN HURT YOUR FEELINGS WITHOUT YOUR COOPERATION AND WILLINGNESS.

No one can cause you to have any kind of emotional reaction without your first giving them permission to do so. You alone are responsible for your feelings and emotions. When you know what you plan to do with your life, you will not allow annoying situations to deter you from your goals for long. If you set ambitious goals for yourself and work enthusiastically toward them, you will quickly realize that you don't have time to allow petty annoyances to upset you and keep you from your objectives.

12. IF YOU CALL ON YOUR FRIENDS ONLY WHEN YOU NEED SOMETHING, YOU WILL SOON FIND YOURSELF WITHOUT FRIENDS.

There is a great deal of wisdom in the old saw, "If you want friends, be a friend." Friendship means giving without expecting anything in return. Busy, successful people are not searching for new friends. If you want to be their friend, you must make the effort to befriend them. Let them know that you are interested in them as people, not in what they can do for you, and you may find that you have made a true and loyal friend.

13. FRIENDS MUST BE GROWN TO ORDER— NOT TAKEN FOR GRANTED.

Your friends will be what you make them. If you are the kind of friend who freely gives of your time and always shows consideration for others, your friends will be generous and kind. If you are the kind of person who takes your friends for granted, neither giving nor expecting much in return, you will attract friends who exhibit the same qualities. In friendship, like attracts like.

Assess your behavior occasionally to determine what kind of friend you are. Are you the kind of person *you* would like to have as a friend? Do you freely give more than you expect in return, or are you always asking and never giving? Do you take the time to stay in touch, to remember friends' special occasions? When you become so consumed with your own interests that you forget about your friends, you are well on your way to becoming friendless.

14. IF YOU WISH "ACQUAINTANCESHIP," BE RICH.
IF YOU WISH FRIENDS, BE A FRIEND.

There is nothing like money to make you attractive and appealing to others. But, of course, the kind of people who are attracted to you only because of what you can do for them may be acquaintances, not friends. You may have many acquaintances if you become wealthy, but whatever your station in life may be, you will never have true friends unless you are a friend to others. Be very selective in your choice of friends. Choose to associate with positive people who like you for the person you are, who encourage you to be yourself and to be the best you can be.

15. IF YOU MUST LET SOMEONE DOWN, BE SURE IT
ISN'T THE FRIEND WHO HELPED YOU UP
WHEN YOU WERE DOWN.

We all have short memories. We become preoccupied with our own interests and daily cares, and it's easy to lose track of friends. There will always be times when you must choose between what you wish to do and what you must do. When you are faced with such decisions, make sure you always remember those true and loyal friends who were there when you needed them, and never, under any circumstances, abandon them.

When you let down a friend who helped you when you needed it most, you will not only adversely affect the friendship; you will seriously damage your own self-respect. When you fail a friend, regardless of how heavy your own burdens may be, you also fail yourself. If you absolutely cannot do what good friends would like, find another way to make it up to them.

16. A FRIEND IS ONE WHO KNOWS ALL ABOUT YOU AND STILL RESPECTS YOU.

A true friend is a priceless gift. When we reveal our hopes, our dreams, and our deepest secrets to others, and they still like and respect us, such people are to be cherished. All too often, the only reason others wish to spend time with us—to be our friends—is because of what they perceive we can do for them, not the other way around. A real friendship is reciprocal, one in which each friend benefits equally.

You can earn the friendship of others by being the kind of person who deserves respect from friends. When others look up to you, it should make you even more conscious of the responsibility you have to treat them with the same respect you would like them to afford you.

17. FRIENDSHIP NEEDS FREQUENT EXPRESSION TO REMAIN ALIVE.

We are all human with frailties, foibles, and insecurities. We each need to be appreciated for the uniqueness that makes us individual, and we need to be told that we are appreciated. Maintaining friendships requires effort and persistent expression, both in word and deed. Tell your friends often how much you appreciate them. Remember occasions that are important to them. Congratulate them upon their achievements. Most important of all, let them know that you are there for them whenever they need you.

18. FRIENDSHIP RECOGNIZES FAULTS IN FRIENDS BUT DOES NOT SPEAK OF THEM.

True friendship acknowledges imperfections, accepts them as part of our individual makeup, and focuses on our positive aspects instead of expounding upon our faults. Your friends don't like you to comment upon their failings any more than you like them to criticize you. When your friends are discouraged or disappointed in themselves, a word of encouragement will serve much better than a sermonette.

To be the kind of friend you would like to have, be a good listener, offer advice when you are asked for it, and treasure the trust that your friends have placed in you. Praise them for their achievements and sympathize when they fall short, but avoid offering "constructive criticism" or playing devil's advocate. Most of us expect more from ourselves than anyone else ever would, and we are painfully aware of our shortcomings. We don't need to be reminded of them by our friends.

19. A GOOD FOOTBALL TEAM RELIES MORE ON HARMONIOUS COORDINATION OF EFFORT THAN INDIVIDUAL SKILL.

Teamwork is a "cooperative effort by the members of a team to achieve a common goal." The key words in the definition are *cooperative effort*. Without the support of the entire group, no team can long endure. Football players quickly learn that no member of the team can be a star in every play. Most moments of glory are built upon a long series of plays, each won by committed, determined, bone-jarring blocking and tackling.

A winning team is one whose members recognize that when one member of the team is successful, the entire team wins. Conversely, a sure way to develop a losing formula is to create an environment in which team members compete with one another instead of the opponent. When all members give their best in every situation—whether they are carrying the ball or clearing the way for someone else—the team wins and so does each individual member of it.

20. WHEN YOU ASK ANOTHER PERSON TO DO
SOMETHING, IT MAY HELP BOTH HIM AND YOU IF YOU
TELL HIM WHAT TO DO, WHY HE SHOULD DO IT,
WHEN HE SHOULD DO IT, WHERE HE SHOULD DO IT,
AND HOW HE MAY BEST DO IT.

We are all influenced by our background and experience. We perceive instructions in the context of our education, experience, heritage, the culture of our organization, and a number of other variables. Good managers know this, and they make sure that their instructions are clear, concise, and well understood. They also know that they must walk a fine line between conveying adequate instructions and killing workers' incentive by not allowing them sufficient latitude to do their jobs.

You may strike the right balance between instruction and motivation by encouraging employees to participate in setting objectives for themselves and their team, helping them develop a plan for achieving their goals, and by making sure that each individual clearly understands the team's mission and his or her role in achieving it. Suggest that team members check in occasionally to report their progress, then get out of their way and cheer them on to victory.

21. REMEMBER THAT THE TONE OF YOUR VOICE OFTEN
CONVEYS MORE ACCURATELY WHAT IS IN YOUR MIND
THAN DO YOUR WORDS.

In a moment of conflict, a suggestion or compromise can salvage a threatened working relationship. A discouraged employee can be motivated again through a few carefully chosen words. In situations like these, a good manager is looking beyond an immediate situation and acting to preserve a future benefit. But if your voice betrays your own anger, fear, or despair, that emotion, not the wisdom you offer, will be what others remember.

Those who rise to the top in any organization are those who have learned to control their emotions. When you have a leadership position, others will watch you closely for the signals you send. You must learn to manage yourself and all the ways in which you convey messages to others if you want to inspire them and demonstrate that you care about all the members of your team.

22. THERE IS HARMONY THROUGHOUT THE UNIVERSE IN EVERYTHING EXCEPT HUMAN RELATIONSHIPS.

Our universe is characterized by order and harmony, yet we human beings must constantly struggle to achieve the same characteristics in our relationships. In fact, human beings seem to find it unnatural to cooperate with others. Successful individuals are those who have learned to swim against the current, to do the things that others refuse to do. They have learned how to work together for the benefit of the entire group.

Achieving harmony in any relationship—business, personal, or professional—requires work. Take comfort in the fact that you'll accomplish far more working with others than working against them.

23. FRICTION IN MACHINERY COSTS MONEY. FRICTION IN HUMAN RELATIONSHIPS IMPOVERISHES BOTH THE SPIRIT AND THE BANK ACCOUNT.

Discord in any relationship often has unpleasant financial implications, but it is far costlier in human terms. When you are involved in a fractious relationship, physical and mental energy that could be directed toward positive achievements is dissipated needlessly, squandered upon stressful, unproductive activities. Unfortunately, whatever the cause of friction between individuals, it adversely affects each person involved.

When you find yourself in a contentious relationship, there are few acceptable alternatives. You can work out your problems or leave the team. Only you know which is the best solution for you, but if you objectively evaluate your reasons for becoming involved and find that they are still valid, your best course of action may be to swallow your pride and find a solution that is acceptable to everyone involved. If you cannot do this, perhaps it's time to get out of the partnership and find another course toward your objective.

24. IF YOU CANNOT AGREE WITH OTHERS, YOU CAN AT LEAST REFRAIN FROM QUARRELING WITH THEM.

When you are involved in a dispute with someone else, it may be the only time doing nothing is better than doing something. There's a practical reason for this: When you quarrel with others—even if you win the argument—you place a great deal of unnecessary stress upon yourself. It is impossible to maintain a Positive Mental Attitude when you allow negative emotions such as anger or hate to dominate your thoughts.

No one can upset you or make you angry unless you allow them to do so. Instead of arguing with others, try asking nonthreatening questions such as: "Why do you feel this way? What have I done to make you angry? What can I do to help?" You may find that the entire situation has resulted from a simple misunderstanding that can be quickly rectified. Even if problems are more serious, your positive behavior will go a long way toward helping resolve them.

25. REMEMBER, IT TAKES AT LEAST TWO PEOPLE TO CARRY ON A QUARREL.

It's difficult to remember in the heat of a disagreement that it takes two to quarrel. It may help to remember that no one can disagree with you while you are agreeing with them. This is not to suggest that you should compromise your principles. It is possible, however, to remain true to your beliefs while simultaneously searching for common ground that will enable you to work productively with others who may at first disagree with you.

When others are upset with you or with a situation that involves you, let them know that you understand how *they* feel. Examine the problem from their point of view. What is the source of the conflict? How could it be resolved in a manner that would satisfy the interests of all involved? How have you contributed to the problem? When you try to find solutions instead of attempting to affix blame, others will almost always respond in kind.

26. MUTUAL CONFIDENCE IS THE FOUNDATION OF ALL SATISFACTORY HUMAN RELATIONSHIPS.

Most of us have two basic questions about others when we enter into a relationship. They are: Can I trust you? and Do you really care about me? Depending upon our previous success in partnerships with others—personal or business—the answers may be slow in coming. Confidence in another is often developed gradually as those involved in the relationship commit themselves to each other's success and happiness.

Although trust and confidence are the basic underpinnings of all successful relationships, they are fragile. A relationship that has endured for months or even years can be irreparably damaged by a few unkind words or a single thoughtless act. Don't allow yourself to act in haste or to lose control of your emotions in important relationships.

27. A GOOD FISHERMAN GOES OUT OF HIS WAY TO BAIT HIS HOOK WITH WHAT THE FISH PREFER—WHICH MIGHT NOT BE A BAD TIP FOR THOSE WHO WISH TO SUCCEED IN HUMAN RELATIONSHIPS.

Just as in a conversation it's a good idea to listen more than you talk, it is also wise in relationships to think about the well-being of others more than you think about your own wishes and desires. When you constantly strive to treat others in the same way you would like them to treat you, you become a person whom others like to be around, one who commands their respect, confidence, and loyalty.

When you learn to manage emotions and your ego, and when you learn to always consider the needs and desires of others, it is inevitable that you will "bait your hook" with kindness and consideration, and catch more friends than you can count.

28. THOSE WHO CREATE GOOD FELLOWSHIP AMONG OTHERS WILL NEVER BE SHORT OF FRIENDS.

If you have a friend who goes out of his way to help cement friendships between others, consider yourself fortunate indeed. In today's frantic, mobile, throwaway society, such individuals are exceedingly rare. With the demands placed upon us by our careers, our families, and the hectic pace of daily life, most of us have little time for ourselves, and even less for our friends. Yet we know that friendship freely given and gratefully received is one of life's greatest gifts.

29. ALL ENDURING SUCCESS IS FOUNDED UPON HARMONIOUS HUMAN RELATIONSHIPS.

Most of us are incapable of "going it alone." Whether it is in our careers, our personal relationships, or in life, we all need others if we are to achieve the level of success we desire. Besides, what's the point of having it all if we have no one we care about to share it? You may choose to work with others, you may ignore them, or you may choose to work against them, but the greatest successes in life come to those who work harmoniously with others. When your personal goals coincide with those of another, not only does the power of your combined labors benefit you, but such cooperation also creates a synergistic effect that allows you to achieve far more than the simple sum of your individual efforts.

30. IF YOU MUST MEDDLE IN HUMAN RELATIONSHIPS, TRY TO BE A PEACEMAKER. YOU WILL FIND THAT YOU DON'T HAVE MUCH COMPETITION.

When faced with a conflict between others, most of us are more inclined to walk away from the situation than to become involved. If we do allow ourselves to become a participant, it is usually by adopting the position of one at the expense of the other. Of course, such behavior does little to resolve the dispute and may in fact exacerbate the problem. But when you make a genuine attempt to help resolve the situation, you should not be surprised if you're the only one.

We are all complex individuals with feelings and emotions we often don't fully understand. Sometimes the mere involvement of a disinterested party is enough to help resolve the dispute. Make sure, though, if you are the one in the middle that you don't allow yourself to get into a position where you must choose between the desires of one person over the other. Work toward a compromise that best suits everyone's interests.

31. UNLIMITED POWER MAY BE AVAILABLE WHEN TWO OR MORE PEOPLE COORDINATE THEIR THOUGHTS AND ACTIONS IN A SPIRIT OF PERFECT HARMONY FOR THE ATTAINMENT OF A DEFINITE PURPOSE.

A Master Mind alliance involves two or more people working together in perfect harmony toward the attainment of a common purpose. Such a partnership creates a superpower that enables each of its members to do far more than either would have been able to achieve separately. Choose your Master Mind partners carefully. Align yourself with people whose strengths complement yours. If you are a right brain person, for example, a logically-driven left brain person may be a perfect counterbalance to your creative bent. Above all, choose to associate only with people who share your positive values and your commitment to similar levels of achievement.

AUGUST

Failure and Defeat

1. EDISON FAILED 10,000 TIMES BEFORE PERFECTING THE INCANDESCENT ELECTRIC LIGHTBULB. DON'T WORRY IF YOU FAIL ONCE.

Arguably America's greatest inventor, Thomas Edison had an extraordinarily positive perception of life that greatly enhanced his ability as an inventor. When others might have been hopelessly discouraged after failing thousands of times in an attempt to develop an electric light, the great Edison simply viewed each unsuccessful experiment as the elimination of a solution that wouldn't work, thereby moving him that much closer to a successful solution.

We could all take a lesson from Edison. Stories abound about inventors who quit trying and gave up too soon or miners who struck gold just a few feet beyond where someone else quit digging. There are few obstacles in life that will not succumb to consistent, sustained, intelligent, positive action. When you are discouraged after you've failed at something, remember Edison's 10,000 failures before he arrived at the solution that forever changed the world.

2. THE AVERAGE PERSON WOULD HAVE QUIT AT THE FIRST FAILURE. THAT'S WHY THERE HAVE BEEN MANY AVERAGE MEN AND ONLY ONE EDISON.

Thomas Edison once observed that the reason most folks don't recognize opportunity when it comes knocking is that it is often dressed in coveralls and looks like work. Edison knew that anything worthwhile never comes easily; if it were easy, anyone could do it. Because he persisted far beyond the point the average person would consider reasonable and rational, he produced inventions that even the most learned people of the day considered impossible.

Great advances in knowledge are often achieved by people with an almost fanatical devotion to finding the solution to a problem. Flashes of inspiration alone are not enough to ensure success; they must be followed by determined, persistent action.

3. DRIFTING, WITHOUT AIM OR PURPOSE, IS THE FIRST CAUSE OF FAILURE.

Without a plan for your life, it is easier to follow the course of least resistance, to go with the flow, to drift with the current with no particular destination in mind. Having a definite plan for your life greatly simplifies the process of making hundreds of daily decisions that affect your ultimate success. When you know where you want to go, you can quickly decide if your actions are moving you toward your goal or away from it. Without definite, precise goals and a plan for their achievement, each decision must be considered in a vacuum. Definiteness of purpose provides context and allows you to relate specific actions to your overall plan.

4. MAKING LIFE "EASY" FOR CHILDREN USUALLY MAKES LIFE "HARD" FOR THEM IN ADULTHOOD.

Del Smith, the millionaire founder and chairman of Evergreen International Aviation, has often said, "Thank God I was born poor; I learned how to work." Like many others who made it to the top on their own, Smith believes that the greatest gift that can be given to a child is to teach him or her the value of work. It is a gift that can never be lost or stolen. It's a natural desire of parents to give their children material things they didn't have as children. Such generosity, however, often deprives children of the greatest gift you can give them: confidence in their ability to take care of themselves. When you make life "hard" for your children by requiring them to learn the value of work, they will have a far greater likelihood of success as adults.

5. MOST OF US DON'T MIND BEING TOLD OF OUR FAULTS IF THE CRITIC IS GENEROUS ENOUGH TO MIX IN A FEW OF OUR VIRTUES AS WELL.

It's a normal reaction to defend ourselves and our behavior when someone criticizes us—even if we secretly recognize that what we're being told is correct. Those who achieve great success in life, however, are those who have learned to set aside their emotions and learn from others, even when the message is unpleasant. If you find yourself being evaluated by someone else, tell yourself that criticism of some aspect of your performance is not a personal attack. Control your emotional reaction and adopt useful ideas even though you may dislike the manner in which the information is delivered.

6. SUCCESS REQUIRES NO EXPLANATION; FAILURES MUST BE DOCTORED WITH ALIBIS.

The surest way to achieve acceptance in any organization or in any line of work is to be successful. Unfortunately, life doesn't work that way. No matter how carefully you study a subject, no matter how rationally you make decisions, no matter how well prepared you are, you will occasionally make mistakes. Human beings always do. The important thing is to realize that temporary setbacks are not permanent failures. Successful people recognize that we all experience temporary setbacks that require us to reevaluate our performance and take corrective action to achieve success. They know that adversity is never permanent.

7. THERE IS A VAST DIFFERENCE BETWEEN FAILURE AND TEMPORARY DEFEAT.

There is no such thing as failure, unless it is accepted as such. Every defeat is temporary unless you give up and allow it to become permanent. In fact, temporary defeat often makes us stronger and more capable. Each time we try and fail, we learn something that helps prepare us for eventual success.

Only in the classroom is there a single correct answer for every problem. If you try an approach that doesn't work, try something else. When you view adversity as nothing more than a learning experience, your successes in life will far outnumber your failures.

8. YOUR REAL COURAGE SHOWS BEST IN THE HOUR OF ADVERSITY.

Some setbacks are so severe that to give in to them means losing the whole ball game. When he assumed command of the Korean War, Gen. Matthew Ridgeway found his forces pushed far to the south, hard pressed by the invaders. Only a determined decision to hold the lines allowed the American forces to keep from being swept into the sea and to eventually regain all the territory they had lost.

When a defeat strikes, you may not have the time to withdraw and contemplate your mistakes without risking further setbacks. Don't succumb to paralysis. It is important to know at that moment what it is you truly desire and to act to preserve your resources and your hope. If you crumble utterly, you will take a blow to your self-esteem that will be hard to repair.

Instead, stick to your principles, and you will know, at the very least, that you have protected the most important thing you have.

9. THERE ALWAYS REMAINS AN OPPORTUNITY TO MAKE A NEW START.

Though it may not seem so when you first encounter a serious blow, you can never lose two of the most important assets you have. These are the power of your mind and your freedom to use it. Once you have turned them to understanding what laid you low, you can begin forming new plans. You may not have the money you once had; you may lack the allies you had cultivated. But you still have the benefit of a universe that eventually rewards honest effort, as well as gaining the experience of mistakes you will never make again.

Remember, no matter where you are now, whatever you can conceive and believe, you can achieve.

10. MOST FAILURES COULD HAVE BEEN CONVERTED INTO SUCCESSES IF SOMEONE HAD HELD ON ANOTHER MINUTE OR MADE MORE EFFORT.

When you have the potential for success within you, adversity and temporary defeat only help you prepare to reach great heights of success. Without adversity, you would never develop the qualities of reliability, loyalty, humility, and perseverance that are so essential to enduring success. Many people have escaped the jaws of defeat and achieved great victories because they would not allow themselves to fail. When your escape routes are all closed, you will be surprised how quickly you will find the path to success.

11. SUCCESS ATTRACTS SUCCESS AND FAILURE ATTRACTS FAILURE BECAUSE OF THE LAW OF HARMONIOUS ATTRACTION.

In physics, positives attract negatives and vice versa, but in human relationships the opposite is true. Negative people attract only other negative people, while positive thinkers attract like-minded individuals. You will find that when you begin to achieve success more successes will follow. This is the law of harmonious attraction. When riches begin to come your way, you'll be amazed how quickly they accumulate.

Train your mind to visualize yourself acquiring a specific amount of wealth or achieving a certain goal—whatever you most desire. Then use self-suggestion to persuade your subconscious mind that you can achieve your goal, and put your plan into action. When you use the tools that you have at your disposal to prepare yourself for success and visualize yourself as having already reached your objective, you can achieve any reasonable goal that you set for yourself.

12. THE ONE WHO TRIES TO GET SOMETHING FOR NOTHING GENERALLY WINDS UP GETTING NOTHING FOR SOMETHING.

Those who think they can get by in life without providing the same amount of value for value received will eventually find themselves working harder than ever to deceive others and receiving very little in return. Life has a funny way of evening the score. In the long run, you will get in the same measure you give. Spend your time on productive, positive efforts; give generously of your time and talents, and you will stand out from the great multitudes whose primary goal in life seems to be to get something for nothing.

13. PEOPLE WHO GAMBLE FOR MONEY ARE POTENTIAL CHEATERS BECAUSE THEY ARE TRYING TO GET SOMETHING FOR NOTHING.

Anyone who risks his or her wealth upon the fickle whims of chance is usually not the type of person you would like to have for a business partner. They are individuals who are most likely to yield to the temptation to cut corners on product quality, overlook unsafe working conditions, and generally fail to deliver on their promises. It is impossible to get something for nothing for a sustained period of time. The law of compensation is unforgiving in its demands that you get what you deserve. You may feel at times that you deserve better—and you may—but eventually your payback will be commensurate with your efforts.

14. ISN'T IT PECULIAR THAT SOME PEOPLE ARE SO CLEVER AT INVENTING ALIBIS AND SO DULL AT DOING THE JOB THAT WOULD MAKE ALIBIS USELESS?

If folks did their jobs with half the effort and creativity they waste in a vain attempt to deceive others, they could achieve great success at anything. It is tempting at times to emulate those who seemingly get by without working very hard, but those who cheat the company by not doing what they are paid to do will eventually pay the price. They will pay with the loss of their most valuable possession: their reputation. The value of a reputation for honesty and integrity is the difference between a career filled with promise and a life of failure.

15. THE OTHER FELLOW'S MISTAKES ARE A WEAK ALIBI FOR YOUR OWN.

Ralph Waldo Emerson said: "It is easy in the world to live after the world's opinion; it is easy in solitude to live after our own; but the great man is he who in the midst of the crowd keeps with perfect sweetness the independence of solitude." It's easy when you are part of a group to "go along to get along," but when you are able to maintain your own highest standards of integrity—regardless of what others may do—you are destined for greatness.

When you have developed a carefully thought out code of personal conduct, you will never have to ask anyone else what the appropriate course of action should be. You will intuitively know.

16. FAILURE IS NOT A DISGRACE IF YOU HAVE SINCERELY DONE YOUR BEST.

We live in a competitive world that measures success by winners and losers, and insists that every victory creates a loss of equal dimension. If one person wins, it seems logical that someone else must lose. In reality, the only competition that matters is the one in which you compete with yourself. When your standard of performance is based upon being the best you can be—for yourself—you will never lose. You will only improve.

Make it a practice to objectively review your performance from time to time. When you fall short, assess the situation and ask yourself: "Is there anything I would or could have done to change the outcome?" If the answer is "no," if you are satisfied that you've done your best, don't waste time reliving the past. Simply learn what you can from the experience, and then get into action again. If you consistently do your best, your temporary failures will take care of themselves.

17. IF YOU HAVE NO MAJOR PURPOSE, YOU ARE DRIFTING TOWARD CERTAIN FAILURE.

Not having a major purpose for your life is like trying to navigate without a chart. You may eventually get somewhere you like, or you may drift aimlessly, always hoping—but never finding—the place where you would like to be. As you grow as a person, so will your major purpose. It is the natural order of things that, when you reach the top of one mountain, you will look around for higher peaks to climb. In life, either you are moving forward or you are going backward. When you plot your course carefully and thoughtfully, you can ensure that you are going in the right direction.

18. IF YOU DON'T WANT YOUR LIFE TO BE "MESSED UP," DON'T FOOL AROUND WITH THOSE WHO HAVE MESSED UP THEIRS.

It is a peculiarity of human relationships that it is virtually impossible for one individual to have a lasting positive influence upon members of a group of negative thinkers. Usually, it works the other way. You cannot maintain a positive, productive attitude if you spend all your time with negative people. Those who have wrecked their own lives (and usually blame their misfortune on others) are not the kind of people who will help you achieve success in your own life. Choose your friends and associates carefully, and refrain from complaints about your job, your company, or any individual. Spend your time with positive, ambitious people who have a plan for their lives. You will find that their optimism is infectious.

19. HUMAN FAULTS ARE LIKE GARDEN WEEDS. THEY GROW WITHOUT CULTIVATION AND SOON TAKE OVER THE PLACE IF THEY AREN'T THINNED OUT.

Habits are formed so slowly that most of us don't realize what is happening until the habits are too strongly entrenched to be broken. Seldom can one pattern of behavior be eliminated without replacing it with another. It has been said that nature abhors a vacuum and will always find something to fill a void. The best way to thin out the "weeds," or faults in your character, is to identify those traits with which you are dissatisfied and replace them with their positive counterparts. If you have a tendency to lose your temper, for example, find a replacement for your anger. Neutralize it with a positive expression or affirmation such as, No one can make me angry unless I let them. I will not let anyone else control my emotions.

20. REMEMBER THAT THE FAULTS OF HUMANKIND ARE PRETTY EVENLY DISTRIBUTED AMONG ALL OF US.

Why can we so easily overlook in ourselves the faults we are quick to spot in others? It is easy to be objective when it comes to criticizing our friends, family members, and business associates, but it is far more difficult to be honest about our own shortcomings. Only when we recognize that we are all human, with the same faults and failings, do we begin to develop that wonderful quality of tolerance that enables us to accept others as they are and ask nothing in return. Replacing faultfinding with "goodfinding" is never easy. But when you become one who always compliments instead of criticizes, you become the kind of friend we would all like to have.

21. SELF-PITY IS AN OPIATE.

The most insidious problem with drugs is that the human body develops a tolerance for them and requires larger and larger doses to achieve the same effect. The same is true with self-pity. The more you allow yourself to indulge in it, the more you will require. Soon, self-pity will become a habit, one so debilitating that you will rob yourself of all the potential you possess.

Happily, there is a cure. If you truly analyze the situation, most often you will find that the problems that have driven you to pity yourself are mostly of your own creation. It follows, then, that the best person to remedy the problem is the person who created it: you yourself.

22. A WISE MAN WATCHES HIS FAULTS MORE CLOSELY THAN HIS VIRTUES; FOOLS REVERSE THE ORDER.

We all have within us the potential for greatness or for failure. Both possibilities are an innate part of our character. Whether we reach for the stars or plunge to the depths of despair depends in large measure on how we manage our positive and negative potential. It is doubtful that, if left unchecked, your virtues will rage out of control. Unfortunately, the reverse is not true about your faults. Left unattended, faults have a way of multiplying until they eventually choke out your good qualities. The surest way to control your faults is to attack them the moment they appear.

23. FAILURE IS A BLESSING WHEN IT PUSHES US OUT OF A CUSHIONED SEAT OF SELF-SATISFACTION AND FORCES US TO DO SOMETHING USEFUL.

If you carefully study your own life and those of achievers whom you admire, it is an absolute certainty you will discover that your greatest opportunities often occurred during times of adversity. It is only when faced with the possibility of failure that we are willing to deal with radical change and take the risks that lead to great success.

When you experience temporary failure and you know that it *is* temporary, you can capitalize on the opportunities adversity always brings.

24. FAILURE SEEMS TO BE NATURE'S PLAN FOR PREPARING US FOR GREAT RESPONSIBILITIES.

If everything we attempted in life were achieved with a minimum of effort and came out exactly as planned, how little we would learn—and how boring life would be! And how arrogant we would become if we succeeded at everything we attempted. Failure allows us to develop the essential quality of humility. It is not easy—when you are the person experiencing failure—to accept it philosophically, serene in the knowledge that this is one of life's great learning experiences. But it is. Nature's ways are not always easily understood, but they are repetitive and therefore predictable. You can be absolutely certain that when you feel you are being most unfairly tested, you are being prepared for great achievement.

25. YOUR FAILURE MAY PROVE TO BE AN ASSET, PROVIDED YOU KNOW WHY YOU FAILED.

There are a few occasions during our brief time on earth when most of us experience great flashes of insight, great moments of truth that forever change the course of our lives. Most of those experiences result from spectacular failures, not from outstanding successes. It is from the failures that so chagrined and dismayed us that we learn the most lasting lessons. When you are the unwilling recipient of a great moment of truth, extract the useful lessons and then put the entire episode behind you. Learn from your failures, forget about them, and move on to better things.

26. IF YOU DON'T KNOW WHY YOU FAILED, YOU ARE NO WISER THAN WHEN YOU BEGAN.

There's an old adage that those who refuse to learn from history are doomed to repeat it. So it is with our failures. Unless we learn from our mistakes, we are likely to repeat them until we learn from such experiences and correct our course—or give up and accept temporary defeat as permanent failure. Every setback you encounter in life contains valuable information that, if you study it carefully, will eventually lead you to success.

Without adversity, you would never develop wisdom, and without wisdom, success would be short lived indeed. When you make a mistake, say, "That's good! I've gotten that out of the way. I will never do that again." You will no doubt make other mistakes, but they won't bother you nearly as much when you treat them as learning experiences.

27. BEFORE OPPORTUNITY CROWNS YOU WITH GREAT SUCCESS, IT USUALLY TESTS YOUR METTLE THROUGH ADVERSITY.

Adversity provides the resistance necessary to develop the strength to overcome great obstacles. This strength consists of self-confidence, perseverance, and, very importantly, self-knowledge. For if you do encounter a setback, it is a clue to a personal weakness. You may have been hasty in judging a competitor, or you may have been too timid in your vision of what needed to be done. Let adversity be your guide to understanding where you misstepped and which qualities you need to cultivate. No one rejoices in disappointment, but if you are success-conscious, you can turn the situation into a chance for improving your character, an opportunity you otherwise would have missed.

28. WHEN ADVERSITY OVERTAKES YOU, IT PAYS TO BE THANKFUL IT WAS NOT WORSE INSTEAD OF WORRYING OVER YOUR MISFORTUNE.

There are few things in life that are as bad as they seem at first. Dealing with adversity begins with analyzing and accepting your situation for what it is. When you realize that things are not nearly as bad as they might have been, you have taken the first step toward working your way through the problem. It is a truism that you will never be asked to carry a heavier load than you can bear, but it sometimes helps you better appreciate that fact if you volunteer some of your time to help those who are less fortunate than you are.

29. YOU NEVER KNOW WHO YOUR REAL FRIENDS ARE UNTIL ADVERSITY OVERTAKES YOU AND YOU NEED COOPERATION.

Everybody loves a winner, it has been said, but nobody knows you when you're down and out. One of the often unappreciated benefits of adversity is that it accelerates the process of identifying your true friends. Most of us have many acquaintances and associates, but we are indeed fortunate if we have a handful of real friends. You will very quickly identify yours when you ask them for help. The wise individual is the one who, when asked for assistance, recognizes that he may one day find himself in the same situation.

30. DON'T BLAME CHILDREN WHO ARE BAD. BLAME THOSE WHO FAILED TO DISCIPLINE THEM.

Ralph Waldo Emerson once observed, "Our chief want in life is somebody who will make us do what we can." Although children doubtless do not recognize it at the time, they crave discipline, particularly during their formative years. Discipline defines boundaries for them, provides security, and is an active expression of a parent's love. Most important, it prepares them for the challenges of adulthood.

If your childhood was less than perfect, you are in good company. Most of us have experienced difficulties at one time or another, and we all make mistakes from time to time. The good news is that while your environment as a child will have a profound influence upon the person you become, it is not the sole determinant. The person you choose to be is entirely up to you. Only you can decide who and what you will become in life.

31. IF LIFE HANDS YOU A LEMON, DON'T COMPLAIN, BUT INSTEAD MAKE LEMONADE TO SELL TO THOSE WHO ARE THIRSTY FROM COMPLAINING.

Wally Amos, the man whom many consider to be the father of the gourmet cookie industry, has turned lemons into lemonade so often in his life that in his official portrait he holds a pitcher in one hand and a glass of lemonade in the other. A perennial optimist, Amos refuses to acknowledge that obstacles are anything other than stepping-stones to success. In a career that has spanned several decades, he has made it to the pinnacle of success several times, only to lose everything and be forced to start over. But he's never lost faith. "You have to have the trust and faith to let go and not agonize," he says. "Don't waste your time worrying. Worry is not preparation. Analyze the situation and focus on solutions. There is always an answer."

SEPTEMBER

Going the Extra Mile

1. A PEACEMAKER ALWAYS FARES BETTER THAN AN AGITATOR.

In today's "everything is negotiable" society, we are bombarded with messages telling us that we get what we demand, not what we deserve. You may temporarily achieve success by demanding more than your due from others, but it will not long endure. "Squeaky wheels" may initially receive the most attention, but the wise wagon master eventually replaces them. It's easy to create problems and dissension but very difficult to lead others in a spirit of cooperation and harmony. Which type of individual do you think is most valuable to the organization? The greatest rewards in life—both financial and personal—will always accrue to the peacemakers of the world.

2. REMEMBER THAT EVERY TIME YOU GO THE EXTRA MILE, YOU PLACE SOMEONE UNDER OBLIGATION TO YOU.

When you do something to or for another, whether your deeds are good or bad, people feel compelled to "retaliate" in kind. If you are a kind and decent person, you can expect to be treated well in return. If you use others for your own advantage without giving anything in return, you will soon find that they have little use for you. People like working for and with positive, considerate people. Start now to develop the habit of going the extra mile.

3. THE END OF THE RAINBOW IS REACHED ONLY AT THE END OF THE SECOND MILE.

Christ's admonition to the faithful in Matthew 5:41: "And whosoever shall compel thee to go a mile, go with him twain," was in response to the Roman custom of allowing officers to force others to carry their load for a mile. The purpose of the biblical principle, similar to the idea of turning the other cheek, was to make good come from evil. You can add goodness to goodness by rendering beyond what you are asked to do. When you truly believe that the habit of going the extra mile is the only acceptable way to conduct yourself in all your dealings with others, when you are driven by a burning desire to serve your fellow man, you will be rewarded both financially and personally.

4. ONLY THOSE WHO HAVE THE HABIT OF GOING THE SECOND MILE EVER FIND THE END OF THE RAINBOW.

It is a fact of life that most of us try and fail many times before we ultimately achieve the level of success that we desire. You can expect to travel the extra mile many times only to find fool's gold at the end of your rainbow. But you will most certainly miss out on the great riches that await you if you quit trying. A superficial commitment to doing more than expected based only on what you expect to receive will not sustain you in the long term. Great achievement results from a commitment to do the right thing regardless of the consequences, and that commitment will ultimately lead you to the pot of gold at the end of your rainbow.

5. EVERY TIME YOU INFLUENCE ANOTHER PERSON TO DO A BETTER JOB, YOU BENEFIT THAT PERSON AND YOU INCREASE YOUR OWN VALUE.

Someone once said that no one can really motivate anyone else; all we can do is motivate ourselves and hope it catches on. You will probably never know how much you influence others with your behavior. When you always go the extra mile, you will influence those in your circle of friends and acquaintances, your family, your co-workers, and even your bosses to do more and better than they have done before.

Your value to yourself and others is greatly enhanced by your ability to influence others to be happier, more productive people. There are no salary caps or career limits for those who lead others to great heights of success. Such people are simply too valuable.

6. YOU CANNOT MAKE ALL PEOPLE LIKE YOU, BUT YOU CAN ROB THEM OF A SOUND REASON FOR DISLIKING YOU.

Even the most popular people have their detractors. Because we are all different, with differing interests and personalities, it is simply impossible for anyone to be beloved by every individual who knows him or her. If your mission in life is to make everyone like you, great disappointment is in store. But if you are always kind and considerate in your dealings with others, they may not like you, but it will be impossible for them to *dislike* you.

You can cement your relationships with others by making sure that you are a person of character, one who is predictably honest, straightforward, and ethical. When you follow such a code of conduct, you may not be sought out by others who do not share your values, but you will be respected by all who know you. And in the end, self-respect will mean far more to you than mere popularity.

7. THE MOST IMPORTANT JOB IS THAT OF LEARNING HOW TO NEGOTIATE WITH OTHERS WITHOUT FRICTION.

Experts in negotiation handle the process so smoothly that discussions hardly seem like negotiations at all. While the word *negotiation* itself conjures up visions of cigar-chomping adversaries pounding the table to emphasize their demands, the best results are achieved when all the parties involved are able to put themselves in the others' shoes and arrive at an agreement that is beneficial to everyone involved.

Whether you are negotiating a higher salary, a new job, or the acquisition of a company, your chances of success are far greater when you approach the situation positively and with a clear objective in mind. It also helps to understand the motives of others involved and to have in-depth knowledge of the subject under discussion. Finally, approach every topic with an open mind—don't simply try to bully others into accepting your proposal or point of view.

8. A BULL MAY HAVE GOOD QUALITIES, BUT YOU WILL NEVER BRING THEM OUT BY WAVING A RED FLAG IN HIS FACE.

Arousing others is easy—if you don't care what kind of action you inspire. If you wish to create a positive response in others, you do so by example and through the art of gentle persuasion, not by daring them to attack. When you work with others, concentrate on their positive attributes, not on the things they dislike or fear. When you take the time to get to know your associates, to learn about their hopes, dreams, and aspirations, you can determine what motivates them. You can then show them how they can align their goals with yours to work together for your mutual advantage. When you do, everybody wins.

9. REMEMBER, YOU CAN PLACE UNDER OBLIGATION TO YOU ANYONE YOU CAN INDUCE TO ACCEPT FAVORS FROM YOU.

It is a very basic human characteristic that we tend to respond to others in the same way they treat us. They will always remember the kindness you extended, and someday when you need it most, help will appear from a totally unexpected source. The kindness and courtesies you extend to others need not be large and expensive. A kind word, a friendly greeting, or assistance with a favorite project lets others know that you care enough about them to lend a helping hand. When you help another cheerfully and enthusiastically without asking for anything in return, the law of compensation places that person in your debt. You have made a friend who is now interested in your success.

10. THOSE WHO DO MORE THAN THEY ARE PAID FOR WILL SOONER OR LATER BE WILLINGLY PAID FOR MORE THAN THEY DO.

If you consistently do more than you are paid to do—whether you are a professional, an executive, an hourly worker, or an entrepreneur—you will eventually be compensated for far more than you do.

If you give more and better service than those around you, customers will beat a path to your door, and your boss will consider you irreplaceable. With the dearth of outstanding service that exists in the world today, you can instantly differentiate yourself from the competition simply by providing good service.

11. START GOING THE EXTRA MILE AND OPPORTUNITY WILL FOLLOW YOU.

Going the extra mile can give you insight and a good reputation, both of which attract opportunity. Many obvious opportunities are found in places no one else has bothered to venture. If you put in the extra effort to make a good project an even better one, or you get to know your equipment better than anyone else on your shift, you will see things others overlook and be in a position to make use of them.

Leaders who need a job done think first of people they know who will do it well. If other people respect you for the quantity and the quality of your work, you will find yourself advancing past others who regard their jobs as drudgery. For all the extra service that you've rendered, you'll find yourself more than amply compensated by opportunities others never grasp.

12. DON'T PUSH OTHERS AROUND IF YOU HAVE NO BLISTERS ON YOUR OWN FEET.

Good officers lead by example and make sure the troops are cared for before attending to their own needs. When you treat others respectfully and never ask another to do something you would be unwilling to do yourself, you are entitled to the respect of others—and they will freely give it. But you cannot expect others to continue marching until they have blisters on their feet while you ride in the jeep. Leading others means you must be willing to give far more of yourself than you would ever ask from them.

13. THE RICHEST PERSONS ARE THOSE WHO GIVE MOST IN SERVICE TO OTHERS.

Financial wealth is only one measure of success. The truly happy and successful individual is the man or woman who is healthy, financially secure, challenged in his or her career, and is making a difference in the lives of others. It isn't always easy to render service to others. The world is a cynical and dangerous place where others are likely to mistrust your motives. They can be convinced only by consistent, sustained, outstanding service that is enthusiastically and cheerfully offered. In time, even the most cynical individual will come to accept your willingness to go the extra mile if you are sincere in your offers of assistance and in the service you provide.

14. ONLY THE HIGHWAY OF USEFUL SERVICE LEADS TO THE CITY OF HAPPINESS.

Psychologists who study human behavior have concluded that we are happiest when we are striving to achieve success. It is the act of striving, not the successful completion of the task, that provides the greatest psychic rewards. When you strive to achieve success through service to others, you multiply the benefits to yourself, and you ensure that whatever road you choose in life will ultimately lead you to success and happiness.

There is no occupation or profession that will not benefit from a concerted effort to better serve others. But the greatest benefit will be to you, in the form of the self-satisfaction that comes from knowing that you made a difference, that without you others would never have received the service you provided.

15. THOSE WHO DO NO MORE THAN THEY ARE PAID FOR HAVE NO REAL BASIS FOR REQUESTING MORE PAY BECAUSE THEY ARE ALREADY GETTING ALL THEY DESERVE TO EARN.

If you look around you, it will be apparent that there are two types of people in the world: There are those who say, "When this company decides to pay me what I'm worth, then I will do what they want me to do." The second is the person who says, "I'm going to be the best I can be because that's the kind of person I am. I also know that if I consistently give more than expected, I will eventually be rewarded for my efforts." It is easy to see that the positive person contributes most to the organization. Yet, very few people are willing to make the sacrifices necessary to achieve success. Make sure you're a member of that group.

16. SOME INDIVIDUALS APPEAR TO BE "ALLERGIC" TO HONEST WORK, BUT OPPORTUNITY IS EQUALLY ALLERGIC TO THEM.

In any business, profession, or occupation, there comes a time when you have to deliver. You may fake it for a time, pretending that you're giving an honest effort, but eventually you will be measured by your deeds, not by your words. If you are more of a talker than a doer, make a vow today—right now —to change your behavior. You may be able to drift through life if you never do more than you are required to do, but you will never know what you might have achieved if you had only been willing to give a little more. The greatest opportunities always go to those who have an affinity for hard work, not an allergy to it.

17. THE MAN WHO DOES HIS JOB PRECISELY AS HE WOULD DO IT IF HE OWNED THE BUSINESS MAY SEE THE DAY WHEN HE WILL OWN THAT BUSINESS OR A BETTER ONE.

The best-managed companies are those in which management creates opportunities for employees to own a piece of the business through various types of stock-ownership programs. Management has found that when individual employees are also owners, they are more loyal, more creative, and more cost-conscious. They also work harder and are more responsive to customers. If you have the opportunity to participate in employee stock programs, do so. If possible, extend the same opportunity to your employees. If such programs are not available to you, conduct yourself as though you were already an owner, and sooner or later you will be. It is inevitable that when you think like an owner, you will eventually become one.

18. DO YOUR JOB PRECISELY AS IF YOU WERE YOUR OWN BOSS, AND SOONER OR LATER YOU WILL BE.

The American system of free enterprise is based upon the premise that every individual may profit in proportion to his or her labors. In today's hectic, highly competitive, global environment, however, you may feel that you are not adequately recognized and compensated for the contribution you make. The next time you feel overworked, underpaid, and unappreciated, remind yourself that you really *are* in business for yourself. Your product is you.

Are you the kind of employee you would like to have if you were the boss? When you are considering a difficult decision or when you are thinking about how to avoid an unpleasant assignment, ask yourself, If this were my company, how would I handle this situation? When your answer is that you would take precisely the same action you are considering as an employee, you are headed for bigger and better things. You will soon be the boss.

19. DON'T BE SATISFIED WITH BEING GOOD AT YOUR JOB. BE THE BEST, AND YOU'LL BE INDISPENSABLE.

Experts have consistently found that after a certain point, money ceases to be a motivator. Even though you may not yet have reached that point, if you are honest with yourself, you will probably find that money is only one of many considerations. When asked if they would continue doing what they do even though it didn't pay well, most highly successful people reply, "Absolutely. I wouldn't change a thing. I love what I'm doing." One of the surest ways to climb the ladder of success is to choose a job that you would do even if you didn't earn much at it. When you are working because you like what you do, the money will follow. You will become such a rare commodity that others will compete for your services—and pay you handsomely for them.

20. WHEN YOU START GIVING OUT, YOU'LL SOON BEGIN TAKING IN.

There's an old folk song about a thirsty traveler who comes across a pump in the desert. An attached note explains that there's a jar of water buried nearby to prime the pump. *You've got to give before you get,* the note says. It is up to the traveler to decide whether to drink the water from the jar or take a chance that the small amount of water invested will result in an unlimited supply of cold, clear water.

So it is with going the extra mile. You've got to give before you get. You cannot expect to receive generous rewards and then decide what to give in return. You must give freely and have faith that the rewards will eventually come. As clergyman Frank Crain once said, "You may be deceived if you trust too much, but you will live in torment if you do not trust enough."

21. IF YOU HAVE SOMETHING YOU DON'T NEED, GIVE IT TO SOMEONE WHO NEEDS IT. IT WILL COME BACK TO YOU IN ONE WAY OR ANOTHER.

You know by now how important it is to offer service freely to your community without expecting anything specific in return. And you know as well how important are the intangible personal benefits of self-respect and inspiration that accompany such action.

But it is also true that by rendering a public service you have an effect on the values in your community. Your actions are a quiet but steadfast signal to others of the importance of being involved, a sign that success does not require heartless devotion to a cause and a reminder to others of the personal satisfaction you gain from your labor. You will find that you inspire others to similar actions in different areas, creating a ripple effect that extends far beyond what you alone can do. The community in which you live will become a better place, and you will be happier being a part of it.

22. THE SUREST WAY TO PROMOTE YOURSELF IS TO HELP OTHERS GET AHEAD.

When you go out of your way to help others get ahead, it is inevitable that they will reciprocate. When you genuinely wish others well, even though you may feel a little envious that they are advancing faster than you or gaining more recognition, they will respond accordingly. Your good deeds will encourage them to do likewise. You may never know how many people have recommended you for a job, or a promotion, or helped you in some other way because you aided them when they needed it most.

23. IF YOU ARE A SHEPHERD, BE THE BEST AND YOU MAY LIVE TO OWN THE FLOCK.

One of the most wonderful things about life is that we are all unique with different levels of intelligence, interests, aptitudes, and desires. How dreadfully dull it would be if we all wanted to be nuclear physicists—or bakers. But, regardless of the gifts we may have received at birth and whichever skills we may have since developed, we all have the capability to be the best at what we do.

Being the best is strictly a reflection of your attitude and your desire. Whether you are a salesperson, an executive, a secretary, or an assembly-line worker, you have the capacity to be as good as you choose to be. When you become outstanding at what you do, you will discover greatly increased demand for your services. When you become the best in your line of work, you may be asked so often to help other "sheep" that you will soon own your own "flock."

24. THE CLIMB UPWARD WILL BE EASIER IF YOU TAKE OTHERS ALONG WITH YOU.

When you take the initiative, you become a de facto leader whose success will depend in large measure upon your ability to inspire others to work with you. They will follow your lead when they have confidence in you and when they know they will share in your success. Few of us are good enough or lucky enough to achieve great success completely on our own. We need others to help us. When we give more in return than we ever ask of our friends and associates, not only will we be able to accomplish much more in life, but it will also make the entire experience much more enjoyable.

25. WHEN THE GOING IS HARDEST, JUST KEEP ON KEEPING ON, AND YOU'LL GET THERE SOONER THAN SOMEONE WHO FINDS THE GOING EASY.

If you think achieving great heights of success will be easy, you either don't understand at all how the process works or you have your sights set too low. Reaching the top of any field is difficult, time-consuming, and often tedious. The reason it isn't crowded at the top is that most people won't do the things that are necessary to achieve success. They are all too willing to give up when the going gets tough. If you need inspiration to persevere, read the biographies of men and women who have achieved greatness in their lives. You will find that they prevailed because they refused to quit. They continued to toil alone long after the masses had given up and gone home.

26. HAVE YOU NOTICED THAT THE MOST EFFECTIVE WORKER IS GENERALLY THE BUSIEST.

Successful people are busy people. They despise idleness and constantly search for new challenges and better ways to do things. When others discover that you are a thoughtful, helpful, enthusiastic worker, you will soon have more business than you can manage, and you will greatly increase the number of people who have a stake in your success.

The most mundane tasks become much more bearable when you compete with yourself to improve at doing them. When you find faster and better ways to do your job, you also free up time that can be spent in more creative pursuits.

27. THE QUALITY AND QUANTITY OF SERVICE YOU RENDER FIXES YOUR WAGES AND DETERMINES WHAT SORT OF EXPERIENCE YOU ARE GETTING.

The only constraints that you have on your income and advancement potential are those you place upon yourself. If you don't like your position, or if you are unhappy with your salary, do something about it. What can you do to make yourself more valuable to your department or your company? What tasks have not been completed because no one has the time or the inclination to take care of them?

Look around and identify things that need to be done. Don't wait to be asked. If you make it a habit to seek out opportunities, to take on new tasks, you will increase your knowledge about the organization and become such a valued employee that your company can't afford to lose you.

28. THE CHANCES ARE THAT YOUR JOB LIKES YOU PRECISELY AS MUCH AS YOU LIKE IT, BUT NO MORE.

You are the world's greatest expert on your job, and you can make it into what you choose. You may have a job description, but there are few jobs in the world that come with detailed instructions. A job description simply provides a foundation upon which you may build the perfect job for yourself. When you give generously to it, a job responds with a full measure of satisfaction, personal growth, financial rewards, and promise for the future.

If you are in a job you absolutely hate, and you have considered all the alternatives and decided that you will never like your job, find something else. But if you, like most people, dislike a few things about your work, but on balance believe you have a pretty good position, get busy making it the greatest job in the world. In your career, as in life, you *get* in direct proportion to what you *give*.

29. YOU MUST GET BUSY DOING SOMETHING ABOUT GOING THE EXTRA MILE.

It's well and good to feel as though you have changed the attitude with which you render extra service, but if that service is in truth no more than anyone else's, then you aren't doing yourself much good. You need to examine your co-workers and competitors to understand just what it is that will make you stand out. If there are job performance standards, exceed them. If you're fulfilling a contract, make sure you offer more than you promised.

You cannot confine extra-mile service to your work alone. You must make it part of your philosophy for dealing with every person you encounter. Imagine how others will be delighted to find that you are the type of person who not only does what is promised but even delivers more. The true benefit of going the extra mile is in teaching yourself to strive always for better and greater achievement in all that you do.

30. THE GREATEST OF ALL SUCCESS RULES IS THIS: DO UNTO OTHERS AS YOU WOULD IF YOU WERE THE OTHERS.

The Golden Rule is more than a principle of ethical behavior; it is a dynamic force that can work good in the lives of untold numbers of people. When you make it a practice to treat others as though you *were* the others, you spread goodwill among people who, in turn, may be moved to do the same. By their actions, they influence still more people, who generate goodwill among even more people. This force for goodwill increases exponentially and will return to you from totally new sources. The benefit you receive from a good deed performed today by a total stranger may have been a chain reaction from long ago when you observed the Golden Rule in your own dealings with another.

OCTOBER

Your Mind

I. THE MAN WHO DIPPED A CHUNK OF ICE CREAM IN
CHOCOLATE AND CALLED IT ESKIMO PIE MADE
A FORTUNE FOR THE FIVE SECONDS
OF IMAGINATION IT TOOK TO CREATE
THE IDEA.

We are just beginning to understand the mysterious ways in which the mind works, but successful people have long known how to use the power of creative vision to their advantage. Many "new" ideas are really nothing more than a new combination of two well-known products or ideas. Nevertheless, great fortunes have been built upon such combinations when they are supported by a clever name and marketing campaign.

There is a definite process that you can use to tap into your imagination. In his book *A Technique for Producing Ideas*, James Webb Young identified five steps:

1. Gather the appropriate information.
2. Work the information over in your mind.
3. Incubate the idea in your subconscious.
4. Recognize the "Eureka!" stage when the idea is born.
5. Shape and develop the idea for practical application.

The technique works. Give it a try the next time you're searching for a creative solution to an old problem.

2. CLARENCE SAUNDERS MADE MILLIONS BY BORROWING THE SELF-HELP CAFETERIA IDEA FOR THE GROCERY BUSINESS AND NAMING IT PIGGLY WIGGLY. IMAGINATION PAYS!

The founder of the Piggly Wiggly grocery chain was a low-level employee in a corner grocery when he visited a cafeteria and got the idea that the same techniques could be applied to the grocery business. He was ridiculed by experts, but he was convinced that the idea was a good one. Saunders persevered, and his adaptation of the self-service idea to the grocery business led him to become the father of the modern supermarket.

It is often true that a great idea alone is not enough to achieve success. Implementation may require as much as or more imagination than coming up with the idea originally. Those who study such things, however, report that when you have a really good idea, even if you can't prove it, you will intuitively know that it is good. If you're convinced, stick with it. Others will eventually recognize the value of your idea.

3. THE IMAGINATION IS THE WORKSHOP OF THE SOUL, WHERE ARE SHAPED ALL THE PLANS FOR INDIVIDUAL ACHIEVEMENT.

Before you can build anything worthwhile, you must first create it in your mind. Your mind is not constrained by physical limitations or boundaries. In the workshop of your mind, you can visualize things that have never been. It is said that Albert Einstein visualized how the universe might look if he were riding astride a beam of light through infinity. Then he worked out the mathematics to support his theory of relativity. You can use the power of your imagination to visualize solutions to difficult problems, to develop new ideas, and to see yourself achieving the goals you have set for yourself.

4. YOUR JOB WILL NEVER BE ANY BIGGER THAN YOUR IMAGINATION MAKES IT.

Daniel Burnham, the turn-of-the-century architect and civic planner whose plan for the 1893 Chicago World's Fair had an enormous influence on contemporary civic design, was quoted as saying, "Make no little plans." He knew that to achieve great things we must have grand ideas. If you can imagine it, you can create it. And if you can create in your imagination the job that you would like to have, it is possible to create it in the real world.

5. IF YOU HAVE A BETTER WAY OF DOING ANYTHING, YOUR IDEA MAY BE WORTH A FORTUNE.

In any type of business, the most valuable ideas are those that make money, save money, save time, or improve the way things are done. Every improvement, however slight, is a step in the right direction. Being alert for opportunities to improve things is a function of a positive attitude. It is virtually impossible to think creatively about opportunities when your thoughts are concentrated on the downside risk instead of the upside potential. As you search for ways to improve your performance, or to find a better, faster, or more economical way to perform a task or build a product, by all means analyze and minimize the risks but focus on the possibilities.

6. THE MIND GROWS ONLY THROUGH USE, AND IT ATROPHIES THROUGH IDLENESS.

Just as the physical body becomes strong through regular exercise, so does the mind require regular use to remain strong. Make sure that your personal development plan includes plenty of mental stimulation. One of the best ways to develop your imagination and visualization skills is through reading. As you read, your mind translates the words into images that help you better understand the concepts about which you are reading. Become a voracious reader. Read newspapers, trade magazines, self-help books, and novels; all will contribute to your store of knowledge and to your ability to visualize and more effectively use your imagination.

7. THERE IS SOMETHING ABOUT TRUTH THAT MAKES IT EASILY RECOGNIZABLE BY ALL WHO ARE SEARCHING FOR IT WITH OPEN MINDS.

Cookie mogul Wally Amos is fond of quoting the saying, "The mind is like a parachute. It functions best when opened." When you open your mind to the possibilities, objectively analyze information and refuse to allow your personal preferences and biases to influence your judgment, you will be able to perceive great truths that have been overlooked by others. A closed mind, though, will cause you to miss out on some of life's greatest offerings.

If you find yourself disputing the facts, or if you keep attempting to revise them to support your beliefs, ask yourself, Why am I so unwilling to accept this information? Am I being logical, or am I simply allowing my emotions to cloud my judgment? The worst mistake you may ever make is trying to persuade yourself to accept a false truth. It is inappropriate to try to fool others, but when you fool yourself, disaster is sure to follow.

8. A CLOSED MIND STUMBLES OVER THE BLESSINGS OF LIFE WITHOUT RECOGNIZING THEM.

To the untrained eye, a geode looks pretty much like an ordinary rock. But a trained geologist knows that inside the geode there is a beautiful crystal lining. The story is the same for those who refuse to examine new possibilities because their minds are closed. Life's greatest opportunities, like the geode, often come in ordinary packaging.

Do not allow yourself to become such a creature of habit that you simply go through the motions and let life happen to you. Just taking a new route to work, putting together a jigsaw puzzle, reading a newspaper instead of watching television, or visiting a museum at lunchtime will stimulate your thought processes and may help you open your mind to new possibilities.

9. TAKE POSSESSION OF YOUR OWN MIND, AND YOU MAY SOON MAKE LIFE PAY OFF ON YOUR TERMS.

Your mind is unquestionably your most valuable possession. You may lose every material thing you own, but knowledge can never be taken from you. With it, you can earn a new fortune, build a new home, and buy anything you truly desire. No one else can control your thoughts; even the cruelest tyrant cannot force you to think about something you refuse to accept. When you make a deliberate decision to take control of your mind and feed it positive, constructive thoughts, you are on your way to taking control of your life. The thoughts you allow to dominate your mind will determine what you will get from life.

10. REMEMBER THE MIND GROWS STRONG THROUGH USE. STRUGGLE MAKES POWER.

Napoleon Hill liked to tell a story about his grandfather, a wagon builder in North Carolina. When the old man cleared the land for cultivation, he always left a few oak trees in the middle of the field at the mercy of the elements, unsheltered by other trees in the forest. It was from those trees that his grandfather made the wagon's wheels. Because they were forced to struggle against the fury of nature, they grew strong enough to bear the heaviest load.

Welcome difficult challenges, for the greatest opportunities will come from challenges that force you to expand your mind as you search for creative solutions. During life's bleakest hours, take solace in the fact that you are strengthening yourself through struggle so that in the future you will be prepared to take on even greater challenges. Like the old oak tree, you grow strong only when you are forced to struggle.

11. BEWARE OF HE WHO TRIES TO POISON YOUR MIND AGAINST ANOTHER UNDER THE PRETENSE OF HELPING YOU. THE CHANCES ARE A THOUSAND TO ONE HE IS TRYING TO HELP HIMSELF.

South African poet and painter Breyten Breytenbach tells of a Black man named Freedom who was the property of a one-legged slave owner in the days before the abolition of slavery. Whenever the owner bought a new pair of shoes, he gave the left one, which he couldn't use, to Freedom. Eventually, wearing two left shoes deformed Freedom's right foot, and he was permanently crippled by the "generosity" of his master.

Don't be fooled by people who attempt to further their own interests under the guise of helping you. Listen to advice from others, thank them for their interest, and make up your own mind about what is best. Follow their advice if it fits with your plan for your life, but don't hesitate to discard it if it doesn't. In all the world, there is only one individual who knows what is best for you, and that person is you.

12. THE KEENEST MINDS ARE THE ONES THAT HAVE BEEN WHETTED BY PRACTICAL EXPERIENCE.

Theoretical knowledge without practical experience might be compared to a large mass of undirected energy. Until it is focused, it is difficult to direct the energy to a useful end. Practical experience is the lens through which the energy of knowledge may be focused and directed toward activities that will provide the greatest benefit.

When you learn new concepts or have an idea that has not yet been tested, make it a practice to think through its application carefully before implementation. When you have considered the possibilities, and it still seems to be a good idea—get into action. The only way to get practical experience is to get to work executing your idea.

13. A QUICK DECISION USUALLY DENOTES AN ALERT MIND.

Successful people are decisive. They don't agonize over decisions and thereby miss out on a great opportunity. They gather the relevant information, discuss alternatives with advisers whose opinions they respect, and then make a decision and get on with it. Indecision creates the worse kind of paralysis and, left unattended, can permanently damage you and your organization. If you have trouble making decisions, remember that there are few decisions that are irreversible. If you later discover that you were wrong, correct your course and move on.

14. CONTROL YOUR OWN MIND, AND YOU MAY NEVER BE CONTROLLED BY THE MIND OF ANOTHER.

The mind is the most powerful weapon known to man. It simply cannot be controlled or contained by an outside force, however formidable that force may at first appear. Throughout history, tyrants have tried to control those who opposed them, but eventually these rulers discovered the power of the imagination was far greater than the threat of the sword. As Victor Hugo said, "An invasion of armies can be resisted, but not an idea whose time has come."

15. THE MIND SERVES BEST WHICH IS USED MOST.

Do you have a continuous improvement program for your most valuable asset—your mind? Make sure that you spend at least a half hour each day studying, thinking, and planning. Review your long-, intermediate-, and short-term goals, and measure your progress to date. Are you on schedule for their completion? Ask yourself, What information do I not have that would help me achieve my goals? Then gather the information you need and get into action.

16. THE MIND NEVER BECOMES TIRED, BUT SOMETIMES IT BECOMES BORED WITH THE "FOOD" IT GETS.

Computer experts use the acronym GIGO—garbage in, garbage out—to illustrate the fact that the computer can process only the information it is given. The same is true with your mind. If you feed it healthful, nourishing "food," it will grow strong and agile, but if you restrict it to a regular diet of mental "junk food," your mind will become unhealthy, negative, and unproductive. It will return to you what you put into it. Feed your mind a balanced, nourishing diet. Study information from a variety of fields to help you keep up with the latest trends. You may find that the best ideas for your business come from a totally unrelated area.

17. KNOW YOUR OWN MIND, AND YOU WILL BE AS WISE AS THE SAGES.

When you take charge of your mind, you take charge of your life. When you understand your thoughts, feelings, emotions, and desires, you can direct them to any end you choose. Wisdom comes from taking the time to study yourself, to know why you are the person you are.

Taking charge of your mind is a thoughtful, reflective, solitary process. Only you can come to understand the complex inner workings of your own mind, and you must be willing to spend the time and effort that gaining such insight requires.

18. IF YOU KNOW YOUR OWN MIND, YOU KNOW ENOUGH TO KEEP IT ALWAYS POSITIVE.

You may not fully understand the complex process that causes electricity to be generated and transmitted to your home. But you understand very well how to apply and use it to illuminate your home, power your computer, and perform hundreds of other essential tasks. The same is true of your mind. No one understands the incredibly complex workings of the brain; we know only that when we use our mind in a certain way, we achieve a desired result. If we think positively, we achieve positive results.

19. NO ONE HAS YET DISCOVERED THE LIMITATIONS OF THE POWER OF HIS OWN MIND.

Pat Ryan, the chairman and CEO of Aon Corporation, the giant multinational insurance company, is fond of saying, "You can't conceive how high 'up' is, except for the limitations of your own mind." It's not very good English, he admits, but it emphatically makes the point that the only limits that can be placed on the power of your mind will be those you impose on it yourself.

When you brainstorm, don't allow limits to be placed on any idea. Sometimes the ideas that seem the craziest at the time will later prove to be the most inspired. If you're working with your Master Mind group, encourage the free flow of ideas from every individual present. Don't be critical or analytical during the brainstorming process; at this point, every idea is a good one. Cluster the ideas into groups of related thoughts so that the best of them can later be shaped for practical application.

20. A NEGATIVE MIND NEVER ATTRACTS HAPPINESS OR MATERIAL SUCCESS, BUT IT WILL ATTRACT THEIR OPPOSITES.

You may trick yourself into believing that you are only playing devil's advocate or searching for weaknesses in apparently good ideas, but in the end negative thinking always produces negative results. Just as your mind will work tirelessly to translate your positive thoughts into their physical equivalent, it will work equally hard to create negative results when all of your thoughts are negative.

21. EVERY BRAIN IS BOTH A BROADCASTING STATION AND A RECEIVING STATION FOR THE VIBRATIONS OF THOUGHT.

Whatever the actual science of thought transmission may be, it is true that if you wish to receive the power contained in the thoughts of others, you must condition your mind to receive those ideas. Listening helps condition your mind to receive valuable information contained in the thoughts of others. Set aside any preconceived notions you may have about the topic, and listen attentively and nonjudgmentally to what is being said. Focus on the information, not on the speaker. Try to identify key concepts behind the speaker's words. Train your mind to identify and absorb information that others often miss because their "receivers" are not tuned to the proper frequency.

22. YOUR TRUE AGE IS DETERMINED BY YOUR MENTAL ATTITUDE, NOT THE YEARS YOU HAVE LIVED.

The American clergyman and author Tyrone Edwards said, "Age does not depend upon years, but upon temperament and health. Some men are born old, and some never grow so." No doubt you've known teenagers who were old before their time and seventy-year-olds who had the temperament and enthusiasm of those discovering the wonders of life for the very first time. It is all a matter of attitude.

As you grow and develop, make sure your experience is directed toward the acquisition of wisdom, not the acceptance of cynicism. If you find it difficult to keep an open mind because of previous experiences, remind yourself that you're dealing with different people, that conditions have changed, or that because you are older and wiser, your chances of success are greater than in the past.

23. YOUR MIND IS THE ONLY THING YOU CONTROL EXCLUSIVELY. DON'T GIVE IT AWAY TOO FREELY THROUGH USELESS ARGUMENTS.

You may spend your time and your energy—both physical and mental—in pursuits that yield the greatest return on your investment, or you may fritter it away on activities that will never bear fruit. Since your mind is entirely your own domain, you may choose to use it to constructive ends, or you can waste mind power—and time—on useless arguments that go nowhere. There is a vast difference between a spirited intellectual debate and a petty argument. When you discuss concepts, your own knowledge is expanded through the interaction with another thinking person. When you allow yourself to be dragged into arguments about insignificant things, the result will be a dulling of both the mind and the spirit.

24. CHICKENS COME HOME TO ROOST, AND SO DO YOUR THOUGHTS. BE CAREFUL WHAT SORT OF THOUGHTS YOU SEND OUT.

The thoughts you send out to others will have a far greater impact upon you than upon them. Unlike a material possession, when you release a thought or give it to someone else, it also stays with you. It may remain buried in your subconscious long after your conscious mind has forgotten about it. Like chickens that return to the coop at night, such thoughts may flash into your consciousness when you least expect them. When your thoughts are positive, you never have to worry about the damage you may do to yourself through negative thinking. Cheerful, productive, happy thoughts that are buried in your subconscious bring positive results when they recur, and by their presence they encourage the maintenance of a positive attitude in all that you do.

25. YOU ARE MORE APT TO "RUST" OUT YOUR BRAIN FROM DISUSE THAN YOU ARE TO WEAR IT OUT FROM USE.

Unlike a mechanical device that eventually wears out and must be replaced if it is used continually and consistently, the mind grows only stronger when it is active. The more you exercise and stretch your brain, the more proficient it becomes. Disuse, however, will have the same effect upon your mind as it will upon a machine. The most intricate, most powerful machine in the world and the greatest minds will rust away unless they are used.

Unless you manage your schedule to permit time for study and learning, it is easy to yield to the temptation to spend your free time in thoughtless, mind-numbing, escapist pastimes. Relaxation is important, but so is gaining new knowledge. Make sure your daily schedule includes an allotment of time for both.

26. SOME PEOPLE ARE NEVER FREE FROM TROUBLES, MAINLY BECAUSE THEY KEEP THEIR MINDS ATTUNED TO WORRY. THE MIND ATTRACTS WHAT IT DWELLS ON.

Worry serves no useful purpose and can have a serious adverse effect upon your mental as well as your physical health. Charles Mayo, who with his brother William founded the famous Mayo Clinic in Rochester, Minnesota, said, "I have never known a man who died from overwork, but many who died from doubt."

Because worry is directed at some vague, uncertain threat, it is difficult to deal with it logically. The best way to get rid of your worries is to take positive action to eliminate their source. When you develop a plan for dealing constructively with problems and get to work implementing your plan, you will no longer be troubled by worries. Negative thoughts al-

ways yield the right of way to a determined person in pursuit
of a positive plan of action.

27. THE WORST THING ABOUT WORRY IS THAT IT ATTRACTS A WHOLE FLOCK OF RELATIVES.

Worries, like sheep, seem to flock together. One worry leads
to another, and soon you are overwhelmed with the potential
for problems. When you allow yourself to play the "what if?"
game—to speculate about additional problems that one potential problem might cause—worries multiply, each making the
next seem worse.

If you must play the "what if?" game, play it to win. Focus
on solutions, not on the problems themselves and the additional problems they might create. However serious your worries may seem when they awaken you at midnight, if you
analyze them carefully, you will find that every problem has a
solution.

28. IF YOU CAN'T MANAGE YOUR OWN MENTAL ATTITUDE, WHAT MAKES YOU THINK YOU CAN MANAGE OTHERS?

Why is it that often those who believe they would be the best
managers of others—if they were only given the opportunity
—haven't learned to manage themselves properly? Before you
can ever have any hope of managing others effectively, you
must first learn to set an example for others to follow. It is
simply impossible for you to inspire others to high levels of
achievement if you cannot inspire yourself to do the same.
Don't make the mistake that many others make by saying,
"When they make me a manager, I'll show them I can manage." The first move is yours. You must first prove yourself
worthy.

29. YOU CAN THINK YOUR WAY INTO OR OUT OF ALMOST ANY CIRCUMSTANCE, GOOD OR BAD.

No action takes place unless it is preceded by thought. If you're unhappy with the circumstances in which you find yourself, you can improve your situation through the power of thought, just as surely as you can destroy a positive life with negative thinking. Success begins with an honest analysis of your present condition, acceptance of responsibility for your own life, and the development of a workable plan to achieve what you desire.

30. A POSITIVE MIND FINDS A WAY IT CAN BE DONE. A NEGATIVE MIND LOOKS FOR ALL THE WAYS IT CAN'T BE DONE.

Someone once said, "There are no truths; there are only perceptions of truth." Whether or not you accept this statement, whatever you believe to be true will become your reality. Your subconscious mind will believe anything you tell it—if you repeat the words often and with conviction. When you are faced with a daunting task that you've never attempted before, focus on the potential for success, not on the possibilities for failure. Break the job down into smaller elements and tackle each one separately. The only difference between success and failure in any job is your attitude toward it.

31. WISE PERSONS ARE THOSE WHO THINK TWICE BEFORE SPEAKING ONCE.

Perhaps the greatest quality in a leader and the most valuable skill in building relationships is the ability to think before you speak. If you have a tendency to speak hastily in anger and regret your actions at leisure, the childhood admonition to count to ten before speaking will still serve you well. When you pause—if only for a moment—to consider the consequences, you may think better of what you were about to say. And if you must speak strongly, it's a good idea to sugarcoat the words—just in case you have to eat them later.

NOVEMBER

Health and Happiness

1. YOUR MENTAL ATTITUDE IS THE MOST DEPENDABLE KEY TO YOUR PERSONALITY.

Your view of yourself will greatly influence how others perceive you. If you are a confident, cheerful, positive person, your co-workers, friends, and family will be attracted to your personality. If you are unhappy, negative, and always complaining about your situation, others will be repelled. Even when at times you don't feel very happy, by forcing yourself to behave in a positive fashion, you will find that you soon feel genuinely upbeat, because your subconscious mind doesn't know the difference between an artificial emotion and the real thing. When you behave positively, you will positively influence everyone around you—including yourself.

2. YOU CAN'T CONTROL OTHERS' ACTS, BUT YOU CAN CONTROL YOUR REACTION TO THEIR ACTS, AND THAT IS WHAT COUNTS MOST TO YOU.

No one can make you feel any negative emotion—fear, anger, or inferiority—without your express permission. There will always be people who find perverse enjoyment in upsetting others, or who simply play upon your emotions so that they can use you for their own selfish purposes. Whether or not they are successful depends entirely upon you and how you react to their negative behaviors.

When you are forced to deal with such people, recognize from the outset that they are trying to upset you, not because of something you may have done to them, but because of some problem they have with themselves. Tell yourself: "This isn't about me. I will not allow this person to upset me. I am in control of my emotions and my life."

3. YOU CAN ALWAYS SEE IN OTHERS WHATEVER TRAITS OF CHARACTER YOU ARE LOOKING FOR.

Margaret Wolfe Hungerford said, "Beauty is in the eye of the beholder." It was her way of saying that we see what we wish to see in others. Every living human being is a complex combination of feelings, emotions, and thoughts—some good, some bad. Your impression of another depends far more upon you and your *expectations* of that person. If you believe someone is good, you will find good qualities. If you don't, you won't.

When you are yourself a positive person, you tend to find positive qualities in others. As you work to develop good, constructive habits to improve yourself continually, make it a practice to look for those same qualities in others. It's easy to spot another's shortcomings, but when you identify the good in others and congratulate them upon their positive achievements, you will make friends on whom you can always depend—both in good times and bad.

4. THERE IS ALWAYS A SHORTAGE OF PEOPLE WHO GET THE JOB DONE ON TIME WITHOUT EXCUSES OR GRUMBLING.

If you really study those who have reached the top of any organization, you will find that they are the people who cheerfully accept challenges, take the initiative, and get the job done. They don't complain, and they don't make excuses. Those who never get anywhere in their jobs and careers can't seem to understand that achievers don't become achievers after they reach the top. They reached the top because of the way they conducted themselves along the way.

You can easily become one of those individuals who regularly advance in the organization—if you are willing to pay the price. Any good manager will tell you that the type of people who are most in demand are those who can think for themselves, who will take the initiative to do the right thing without being told, and who will stick to the job until it is finished. You can be one of those people if you choose to be.

5. HOW CAN YOU JUDGE OTHERS ACCURATELY IF YOU HAVE NOT LEARNED TO JUDGE YOURSELF ACCURATELY?

The ability to evaluate yourself and your performance objectively is critical to your relationships with others and will have an enormous impact upon the level of success you achieve during your lifetime. Unless you can honestly evaluate your strengths and weaknesses, how can you ever expect to improve your performance? You must determine where you are before you can develop a plan to get you where you would like to be.

If you were an independent, dispassionate observer, what advice would you give to yourself to improve your skills, your work habits, your interaction with others, and your contribution to the organization? Honesty about yourself is the first step toward self-improvement.

6. DID YOU CHEAT THE OTHER FELLOW OR YOURSELF? THINK CAREFULLY BEFORE YOU ANSWER.

When you are dishonest in your dealings with others or when you take advantage of them, you cheat yourself more than you cheat them. They may regret their dealings with you for a time, but they will eventually get over it and move on to other things. You, on the other hand, must live with your behavior for the rest of your life. In your heart, you will know the truth about what kind of person you are.

Everyone is occasionally tempted to take advantage of others. If they are dumb enough to get themselves into this situation, the thinking goes, they deserve what they get. In reality, however, when you are fair and honest with a person of whom you could have taken advantage, you become a better person.

7. THE THREE MOST COSTLY WORDS IN THE ENGLISH LANGUAGE ARE "I HAVEN'T TIME."

The costs from these words are manifold. You can lose the pleasure of time with your family. You can fail to correct a small error that will compound itself later. You can ignore your body's pleas for rest and exercise. Whatever the instance, do not allow a supposed lack of time to prevent you from doing the things that preserve your happiness.

There are many ways to organize your time better so that you have the freedom to do what needs to be done. A good leader always has a trusted associate to carry part of the burden during a difficult period, and anyone can turn to PMA to find the energy to do a job faster and better. If you're constantly pressed for time, you may need to engage in a wholesale analysis of the way you work, but never let the lack of a few minutes hold you back from anything you want or need to do.

8. HAPPINESS CAN BE MULTIPLIED BY SHARING IT WITH OTHERS WITHOUT DIMINISHING THE ORIGINAL SOURCE. IT IS THE ONE ASSET THAT INCREASES WHEN IT IS GIVEN AWAY.

With happiness, the more you give, the more you get. The greatest rewards in life do not come from the accumulation of financial assets; they result from the psychic gratification that accompanies helping others achieve happiness. Those who acquire the greatest riches in life have discovered how to link the two; they have learned how to provide a service that creates satisfaction for customers and generates profits for themselves.

When you approach your job with exuberance and a determination to make your customers glad they chose to do business with you, great benefits will accrue to you. There are never enough happy people who share their joy with others.

9. A SMILE IS A LITTLE THING THAT MAY PRODUCE BIG RESULTS.

In the animal kingdom, baring one's teeth is a sure sign of aggression, but in the world of humans, the opposite is true. Nothing disarms an angry or aggressive person faster than a heartwarming smile. A ready smile will ensure that the welcome mat will always be out for you, and when your request for assistance is accompanied by a smile of genuine friendship, you will soon have more help than you need.

Practice smiling at others until it becomes a natural reaction to flash a friendly smile at those with whom you come in contact—when you're introduced to someone, when you greet an old friend, or when you arrive at work each morning. Make sure, however, that your smile is genuine. Others can quickly spot a fraud, and nothing turns people off more quickly than a phony smile that has no real feeling behind it.

10. HAPPINESS IS FOUND IN DOING— NOT MERELY IN POSSESSING.

It's true. Money can't buy happiness. Most of us are motivated by aspirations of the *lifestyle* we desire for ourselves and our families, not by the physical possessions—homes, vacations, automobiles, etc. When you recognize this fact, you will know that you must constantly "raise the bar" to encourage yourself to reach higher goals. Your goals should include the possessions that you desire, but as former Apple Computer chairman and CEO John Sculley said, "Success is a journey, not a destination. Make sure you enjoy the trip."

11. YOU CAN'T FIND HAPPINESS BY ROBBING ANOTHER OF IT. THE SAME APPLIES TO ECONOMIC SECURITY.

There are few things in this world that will enrich your life if you deprive other people of them. Usually the reverse is true. When you share your wealth and happiness, you improve your own share of both. In fact, neither happiness nor economic security is of great value unless it is shared. Happiness cannot be hoarded and saved until it is needed, and security is an abstract concept. As Gen. Douglas MacArthur once observed, "There is no security in life. There is only opportunity." You must find happiness and economic security for yourself, and share them to keep them.

12. A SMILE HELPS YOUR LOOKS, MAKES YOU FEEL BETTER, AND COSTS NOTHING.

It's a natural reaction when we face a camera to flash a smile. We instinctively know that we are more appealing and attractive when we are smiling. When you smile at others, it elicits a favorable reaction from them, but most important, it makes you feel better as well. It's not all psychological. Experts have found that when you smile, your body chemistry changes and you actually do feel a sense of happiness and well-being.

When you keep a smile in your voice, others drop their defenses and open up to you—in person or on the telephone. Workers who spend much of their time talking on the telephone have learned that people they converse with can "hear" the smile in their voice. If you have trouble remembering to keep a pleasant tone of voice, keep a small mirror beside your phone so you can check your smile while you speak.

13. ANY PERSON CAN BE WON BY AFFECTION QUICKER THAN BY HATRED.

The best way to get someone to like you is first to like him or her. You will find that it is virtually impossible for someone whom you like not to like you. Human beings simply aren't made that way. Whatever ill feelings others may have toward you will immediately dissipate in a single expression of admiration from you to that person. When you realize the wisdom contained in this concept, every person you meet is a potential friend.

The surest way to win affection is to give it—freely and without reservation. If you attach conditions to your friendship or attempt to win others to your cause simply because of what they can do for you, they will quickly sense your insincerity. When you demonstrate by your actions that you care about them, and you always give more in return than they give to you, they will be your friends for a lifetime.

14. THOSE WHO GIVE FREELY OF HAPPINESS ALWAYS HAVE A BIG STOCK OF IT ON HAND.

As the American educator William L. Phelps noted, "Real happiness is not dependent on external things. The pond is fed from within. The kind of happiness that stays with you is the happiness that springs from inward thoughts and emotions. You must cultivate your mind if you wish to achieve enduring happiness. You must furnish your mind with interesting thoughts and ideas. For an empty mind seeks pleasure as a substitute for happiness."

15. YOU CAN LAUGH OFF WORRIES THAT YOU CAN'T SCARE AWAY WITH A FROWN.

Some years ago, a well-known magazine editor literally laughed himself back to health. Hospitalized by a debilitating disease and in great pain, he noticed that when he was happy, his physical pain diminished. This observation led him to launch a self-prescribed program of laughter designed to cure himself. He read joke books, told jokes, asked visitors always to come prepared with jokes, and endlessly watched comedies on television. He won his battle with the disease.

Don't take yourself so seriously that you cannot laugh at yourself or your situation. You will never be able to work the more than 80,000 hours (40 hours a week for 40 years with two weeks' vacation) that will be expected of you during your lifetime unless you figure out how to have a little fun along the way.

16. WHEN YOU FEEL SLUGGISH, TRY NATURE'S DOCTOR. JUST QUIT EATING UNTIL YOU ARE HUNGRY AGAIN.

Many experts advocate eating four small meals a day, each about the same in nutrition. When you limit your intake of fats and sugars, you needn't worry too much about calories. A diet heavy in grains, vegetables, and fruits is more easily digested, keeps blood sugar more stable, diminishes your appetite, and results in a higher and more constant energy level because there is less fat storage. You will feel more energetic almost immediately when you adopt such a diet.

17. THE BEST TIME TO "DOCTOR" IS BEFORE YOU BECOME SICK.

When it comes to maintaining sound physical health, there is much to be said for preventive maintenance. In fact, many of our most serious health problems—cancer and heart disease among them—can be self-induced. Smoking and poor eating habits have contributed to shortening the lives of millions of people. Unfortunately, the damage occurs over such a long period of time that by the time we feel the effects, it is too late.

Don't allow your health to be ruined by bad habits. Adopt a lifestyle that eliminates all substance abuse and replaces bad eating habits with a healthy diet and plenty of exercise. When you do, you will not only feel better physically. You will feel better about yourself.

18. IF YOU WOULD HAVE GOOD HEALTH, LEARN TO QUIT EATING BEFORE YOU ARE ENTIRELY SATISFIED.

Many of our poor eating habits were developed as children when we were encouraged to be a member of "the clean-plate club," eating everything we were served. As adults, however, our metabolism changes and our needs are vastly different. When we have fully matured, we require far fewer calories to nourish our bodies, so the excess is stored as fat. When we stop growing up, we start growing out.

Eat smaller portions, stop eating before you are fully sated, and chew your food longer. A good dinner companion can help, too. A lively conversation can take your mind off the food you eat and focus you on food for the mind.

19. KEEP YOUR MIND ON YOUR PHYSICAL ILLS, AND YOU'LL ALWAYS BE SICK.

Doctors have just begun to learn the importance of attitude in the maintenance of sound physical health. If you do the things that are necessary to stay healthy and don't worry constantly about what might be wrong with your body, your chances of maintaining good health are infinitely better than if you allow your mind to dwell constantly upon the things that might be wrong with you. You do become what you think about. The mind is a marvelous piece of equipment that can exert great influence upon the physical body. Keep your mind strong and healthy, and your body will benefit as a result.

20. SOME CELEBRITIES ENDORSE FOR A PRICE PRODUCTS THEY WOULDN'T CONSUME AT ANY PRICE.

Perhaps more than at any other time, it is essential for you to exercise good judgment and to use old-fashioned common sense in every decision you make. We live in a world filled with hype and empty promises. Because they are paid a fee for doing so, people you admire sometimes become spokespersons for products they wouldn't touch themselves, but they have no compunction about attempting to persuade you to buy.

When it comes to what you ingest, make your own decisions about what you eat; do not be influenced by those whose self-interest is served by selling something to you. Food manufacturers are required by law to disclose the contents of their products so that you can determine whether or not you wish to consume them. Become an avid label reader.

21. WITH RIPE FRUIT AND RAW VEGETABLES, YOU CAN NEVER OVEREAT.

Evolution may not have taught human beings to find great pleasure in eating foods that are best for us, but our digestive systems haven't fully adapted to handle efficiently some of the things we may like most. It requires a tremendous amount of energy, for example, to digest meats and other heavy foods, energy that could otherwise be directed toward the achievement of something more constructive than simply processing food. It is virtually impossible, however, to eat more raw vegetables and ripe fruit than is good for you. Such foods have little fat content, your body processes them more easily, and they provide nutrients that are quickly transformed into energy.

22. YOU KNOW WHAT TO FEED YOUR AUTOMOBILE FOR GOOD SERVICE; LEARN WHAT TO FEED YOURSELF FOR GOOD HEALTH.

We often go to great lengths to learn how machines work and the type of service they require to stay in good working order. Yet when it comes to our body—the most important possession we own—we pay scant attention to its needs. But it is never too late to learn. There are literally hundreds of books available on the subject. Learn what you need to know, take care of your body, and it will take care of you.

23. DON'T TRY TO CURE A HEADACHE. IT'S BETTER TO CURE THE THING THAT CAUSED IT.

If you have a serious medical problem, by all means see a doctor. But also keep in mind that many of the ailments for which there are thousands of over-the-counter remedies are caused by things you can control. Headaches, an upset stomach, muscle aches, lethargy, and the like are signals that you are ignoring your body's needs or your mind's problems.

Consider carefully whether you've been putting off a worrying issue that causes you tension. Ask yourself whether you're getting the exercise your body needs to stay trim and energetic. As with any adversity, it is important that you act right away to understand the source of your problem and work to correct it. Once you do, you'll find you have more enthusiasm and vigor to pursue your Definite Major Purpose.

24. WATCH YOUR EATING HABITS AND PREVENT A DOCTOR'S BILL.

We are just beginning to understand the far-reaching effects diet has upon our health and well-being, but we do know which foods are good for us and which are most harmful. Still, we often ignore such wisdom, preferring to enjoy ourselves now and worry about the consequences later.

If you pay attention to nutrition, you may avoid other health problems. Experts advise avoiding large amounts of caffeine, alcohol, and salt, and following a low-protein, low-fat diet that is high in carbohydrates such as vegetables, cereals, pasta, breads, potatoes, and fruit. They also suggest plenty of high-fiber foods such as cereals, whole-grain breads, potatoes, and high-fiber vegetables and fruits such as broccoli, carrots, string beans, oranges, and strawberries.

25. A BIG APPETITE GENERALLY DOESN'T LEAD TO SOUND HEALTH.

A common cause of food-related illness and disease is overeating. Diet is one area in which less is definitely better. This is especially true when it comes to foods containing refined sugar. If you find that you are unable to give up sweets entirely, at least limit your intake to one or two small portions per week. Your system will be able to handle minimal amounts; just don't make sweets containing refined sugar a regular part of your diet.

26. TIME IS THE GREATEST OF ALL DOCTORS. GIVEN A CHANCE, IT CAN CURE MOST OF THE ILLS THAT PEOPLE COMPLAIN ABOUT.

This does not mean you should ignore physical problems. If something is wrong with your body, you need to try to understand as quickly as possible what is causing your ailment and then act to correct the situation.

But sometimes we find ourselves tense and aching. Our heads feel fit to burst, our stomachs rebel at the mildest food, and the ache in our backs is relentless. Simple tension can be the cause, and the solution is plain old honest relaxation. Allow yourself time each day to unwind, to contemplate the things you enjoy. A few hours of carefree pleasure each week can do wonders for the problems that plague you and give you the energy and perspective you feel you've lost.

27. THE MAN WHO BUILDS A HOUSE ALWAYS GETS MORE FOR HIS WORK THAN DOES THE MAN WHO TEARS IT DOWN.

In any line of work, in any business, profession, vocation, or calling, it requires far more skill, dedication, and persistence to create something worthwhile than to destroy the creations of others. The vision and craftsmanship that are necessary to construct a thing of beauty—from ordinary materials that are available to anyone—command far greater remuneration than the unskilled labor required to demolish the work. Make sure you are a builder and creator, not a destroyer, of things and ideas. Mostly, it is a matter of attitude. When you make it a habit to search for creative, imaginative ideas, to look for better ways to do the same old things, you will become a builder.

28. WHEN YOU CAN'T WIN, YOU CAN AT LEAST GRIN.

Courage is what Ernest Hemingway described as "grace under pressure." When you can demonstrate good sportsmanship in the face of defeat, you have taken the first step toward earning the respect of your peers and preparing yourself for the next victory. Don't take yourself and your situation so seriously that you cannot give a smile of sincere congratulations to someone who has temporarily bested you. Wish him or her well, then rededicate yourself to improving your own ability—and stay in the game.

29. BEGIN LOOKING FOR SYMPTOMS OF ILLNESS, AND THE DISEASE ITSELF WILL SOON PUT IN ITS APPEARANCE.

The powers of your mind are truly incredible. So profound is its effect on your physical well-being that it is standard practice when testing new medicines to administer a placebo to a control group. If the mind thinks the body is receiving medication that will have a positive effect, recipients of the placebo may actually exhibit the same characteristics as those receiving medication.

Use the knowledge of your mind's influence upon your physical health to your advantage, combining your physical regimen with a positive attitude toward life. If you take the steps necessary to maintain good health, your attitude will be improved, and if you have a positive attitude, you are more likely to adopt a healthy lifestyle. The effect is a synergistic relationship between your physical and mental health. One benefits the other.

30. IF YOUR MIND CAN MAKE YOU SICK—AND IT CAN— REMEMBER THAT IT ALSO CAN MAKE YOU WELL.

You cannot have a healthy body without a healthy mind, and it is exceedingly difficult to maintain a Positive Mental Attitude when your body is unwell. Follow work with play, mental exertion with physical activity, exercise with rest and relaxation, and eating with fasting. And temper seriousness with good humor.

DECEMBER

Faith and Hope

1. MISFORTUNE SELDOM TANGLES WITH THOSE WHOSE BODYGUARDS ARE HOPE AND FAITH.

Did you ever wonder why some people seem to lead a charmed life, that everything always seems to work out for the best for them? If you look a little closer, you may find that appearances are deceiving. The chances are good that they've had just as many problems, setbacks, and failures as anyone else; they have just dealt with them differently. They don't allow themselves to lose hope simply because they have had an unfortunate experience. They have faith that things always work out for the best. When the misfortune is yours, it may be difficult to accept, but you will find that if you refuse to accept defeat, success will eventually follow. As long as you have faith and hope, there is no misfortune that cannot be overcome.

2. FAITH NEEDS A FOUNDATION ON WHICH TO STAND. FEAR EXISTS WITHOUT A BASE.

One of the fundamental tenets of every religion is faith. Unless you are willing to suspend your cynicism and disbelief, it is simply impossible to accept the existence of a Supreme Being. The same is true with your faith in yourself, your abilities, and the god you worship. You must build a foundation of faith to support yourself and your beliefs. When your foundation is strong, you can quickly dispel the fears that attempt to erode your faith.

Unless your foundation is built upon an understanding of the principles in which you believe, it can be destroyed by the winds of doubt and fear that assail us all from time to time.

Make sure you know what you believe and why. When you do, your foundation cannot be shaken.

3. A FREE MAN FEARS NOTHING.

There is no obstacle you will ever face that you cannot overcome as long as you remain free. When you have the freedom of choice to pursue any alternative you wish, your only constraints will be those you impose on yourself. The United States has survived a civil war, two world wars, the Great Depression, a presidential resignation, and assaults upon all of our institutions. We survived because our democratic form of government is based on a belief in the inherent goodness of humankind. It is a system based on optimism and hope, not on tyranny and oppression. Cherish your freedoms, and celebrate your patriotism and loyalty. Be proud that you are a participant in the world's greatest experiment—democracy!

4. YOU CANNOT BE ENTIRELY FREE UNTIL YOU ARE ENTIRELY HONEST WITH YOURSELF.

Self-deceit is an insidious cancer of the spirit. As long as you attempt to deceive yourself about who you are and what you stand for, you will be confined in a prison of your own making. You cannot begin to realize your potential until you acknowledge the person you are and begin to shape yourself into the person you wish to become. The lifelong process of personal growth begins with a commitment to honesty—to yourself.

When you rationalize your failure to do something that you know you are perfectly capable of doing, you erect another barrier to your success. Unless you fully understand your capabilities—and are honest with yourself about them—you will never be free to pursue any goal you choose. You will be held back by doubts and fears that you have created by your unwillingness to assess your performance honestly.

5. FAITH WILL NOT BRING YOU WHAT YOU DESIRE, BUT IT WILL SHOW YOU THE WAY TO GO AFTER IT FOR YOURSELF.

Webster defines faith as "a confident belief in the truth, value, or trustworthiness of a person, idea, or thing, a belief that does not rest on logical proof or material evidence." Faith is an intangible, abstract idea, a willingness to accept something that has not yet—and may never be—proven. Having faith that you can accomplish something will not achieve your objective, but it will give you the courage to do what you must to reach your goal.

There will be times in your life when you cannot prove that your faith in yourself is justified. You must accept the fact based upon your intuitive feelings that you are capable of greatness. No doubt you will be disappointed in yourself when you fail to live up to your expectations. But if you don't have faith in yourself, you will never begin to reach your potential . . . because you will be unwilling to try.

6. AN INDIVIDUAL WHO IS AT PEACE WITH HIMSELF IS ALSO AT PEACE WITH THE WORLD.

Peace is not something that can be bestowed upon you. It can only come from within. Developing inner peace is a lifelong endeavor. As the world around you changes and your relationships with others evolve, your personal security will be threatened. Change—especially that of large magnitude—is always threatening. You can deal with life's vicissitudes far more effectively when you grow in stature in response to life's challenges. As you mature as an individual, make sure your personal improvement program includes nourishment for the spirit as well as for the body and mind.

7. UNLESS YOU HAVE PEACE OF MIND, YOU ARE NOT A FREE PERSON.

Peace of mind is liberating. When you have faith and confidence in yourself, based upon a realistic assessment of your ability to achieve your definite purpose, your serenity cannot be threatened by external forces. You will know that your faith in yourself is justified, and you will be free to pursue any goal so long as it does not violate the laws of God or the rights of your fellow man.

Your spiritual nourishment should include a study of the works of great writers and philosophers. Contemplation of grand thoughts that have been examined by leading thinkers throughout history will help you gain insight into your own feelings and beliefs and enable you to lead a more thoughtful, more fulfilling existence. Only when your convictions are based upon study and introspection can you develop the intellectual security that leads to peace of mind.

8. THE GREATEST AND MOST EFFECTIVE OF ALL PRAYERS ARE THOSE OFFERED AS GRATITUDE FOR THE BLESSINGS WE ALREADY HAVE.

Prayer is the active expression of faith, and it serves as a conduit to the wisdom of the ages. The power of prayer will sustain you when the going is difficult, and it will help you cope positively with success. When you pray, do not ask for more material possessions. Instead, ask for the wisdom to better appreciate and utilize the possessions you already have. When you do, you condition your mind to receive the great power that is available to you, the Higher Power that anyone can draw upon for sustenance.

9. IT IS BETTER TO GIVE THANKS FOR THE BLESSINGS WE ALREADY HAVE THAN TO PRAY FOR MORE BLESSINGS.

The power of prayer has been discussed and dissected by theologians and disbelievers alike since the origins of religion. For the faithful, prayer is the direct line to God; for the disbelievers, it may be nothing more than a method of organizing thoughts and affirming goals. Whatever you believe prayer to be, it is your connection to the mysterious source of power that resides outside the realm of the physical.

Never let a day go by without a prayer of thanks for the bounty you enjoy, no matter how small it is. And go out of your way every day to expend a part of your time and energy in helping others. Remember, too, that no problem is unique or new. You can always seek advice or help. And you are never alone. A Greater Power is with you always. Learn to rely on it.

10. PRAYERS EXPRESSED WITH FEAR OR DOUBT ALWAYS PRODUCE ONLY NEGATIVE RESULTS.

Some years ago, Harvard professor Robert Rosenthal conducted a study in which he told elementary-school teachers that some of their students (who were actually selected at random) were intellectual "bloomers." During the course of the year, 47 percent of the children whose teachers expected them to shine intellectually gained as many as twenty IQ points. Rosenthal called the phenomenon a "self-fulfilling prophecy."

When you doubt that your prayers will come true, it's a good bet you are about to experience the phenomenon of a self-fulfilling prophecy. The mind is constructed so that if fed negative information, it will respond negatively. Always place your prayers in a positive context. If you would like to overcome fear, for example, do not pray for help in dealing with fear. Instead, frame your prayer positively by asking for help in developing courage.

11. THE ART OF BEING GRATEFUL FOR THE BLESSINGS YOU ALREADY POSSESS IS OF ITSELF THE MOST PROFOUND FORM OF WORSHIP, AN INCOMPARABLE GEM OF PRAYER.

Make it a practice to pause for a few moments every day—perhaps just before you go to bed at night—to give thanks. When you pray, do not ask for more blessings; instead ask for wisdom and understanding to make better use of the blessings you currently possess. And ask for greater understanding so that you may occupy more space in the hearts of your fellow men by rendering more and better service to them tomorrow than you rendered today.

12. THE FIVE KNOWN REALITIES OF THE ENTIRE UNIVERSE ARE TIME, SPACE, MATTER, ENERGY, AND THE INFINITE INTELLIGENCE THAT GIVES THESE ORDERLINESS.

The Rev. Bernhardt Fraumann, a Presbyterian minister and *Think and Grow Rich Newsletter* columnist, believes that the order of the universe is one of the most compelling arguments for the existence of God. The universe is simply too intricate in its design to have occurred randomly. He says that the magnificence of the universe is in itself convincing evidence that "God is in the loop." We may not understand the complexities of Infinite Intelligence, but we can tap this spiritual power and put it to good use in our own lives.

13. TODAY'S DREAMS BECOME TOMORROW'S REALITIES. DO NOT BELITTLE THE PRACTICAL DREAMER, FOR HE OR SHE IS THE FORERUNNER OF CIVILIZATION.

At a recent meeting of science fiction writers, the assembled authors wrestled with a particularly interesting problem. For years, it was commonly understood that a good sci-fi writer imagined things that might actually be possible in about thirty years. The problem is that technology is advancing so rapidly that even the most imaginative of the authors found themselves falling far short of the reality that is possible in today's world.

When you reflect upon the possibilities in your business or your area of expertise, allow time for "blue sky" thinking. What might be possible if the factors that currently constrain advancement were eliminated? What trends are likely to affect your business or the way your customers think? What must you do to stay in the forefront of your profession? In your answers, you may find tomorrow's innovations.

14. THERE IS NO SUCH THING AS GOOD OR BAD LUCK. EVERYTHING HAS A CAUSE THAT PRODUCES APPROPRIATE EFFECTS.

There are few absolutes in life. Virtually any action you take can have an effect upon yourself and others that may be either good or bad, positive or negative, depending upon the circumstances. An act that is perfectly appropriate in one setting, for example, might be totally inappropriate at a different time and place. Whether you have good or bad luck depends far more upon your reaction to circumstances than to the circumstances themselves.

W. Clement Stone has often said that a Positive Mental Attitude is the attitude that is appropriate under the circumstances. It is a can-do attitude that manifests itself in positive action, which almost always generates positive results. When you take action in a spirit of positive achievement, your luck will be good even if the results are not what you expected or initially desired. Positive action always eventually creates positive results.

15. THERE IS NO SUCH THING AS PASSIVE FAITH. ACTION IS THE FIRST REQUIREMENT OF FAITH. WORDS ALONE WILL NOT SERVE.

"Applied faith" is the application of your faith in yourself, your fellow man, opportunity, and in God—under any circumstances. Applied faith is an essential component of success. Without faith in yourself, you would be unwilling to attempt anything, and without faith in your fellow man, you would be unable to establish the trust and rapport that are a requisite of doing business with others. And of course, for many, faith in God provides meaning and purpose in life.

16. THE ONLY PERMANENT THING IN THE ENTIRE UNIVERSE IS CHANGE. NOTHING IS THE SAME FOR TWO CONSECUTIVE DAYS.

The Roman philosopher Pliny the Elder wrote in the first century that "the only certainty in life is that nothing is certain." Since before those words were penned, human beings have resisted change, analyzed it, and attempted to control it—all to little avail. To be successful in today's high-tech, fast-paced world requires more than a willingness to accept change; we must learn to welcome it enthusiastically. As Alvin Toffler wrote twenty-five years ago in his bestselling book, *Future*

Shock, those who will be successful in the Information Age will be those who, instead of revolting against change, anticipate and embrace it.

17. TODAY'S WORRIES MAY BECOME TOMORROW'S PRICELESS EXPERIENCES.

How odd many of our worst fears appear when viewed with 20/20 hindsight. The worries that seemed so monumental at the time were somehow dealt with, and we went on to more productive things. In fact, often we later realize that our fears during those moments of terrible, traumatic stress were greatly exaggerated. As time passes, we discover that it was from those very experiences that we gained more penetrating insight into ourselves and what life is all about.

Part of maturity is the recognition that seldom are things as bad as they first appear. Experience teaches us that we can always find a solution to a problem if we take the time to analyze the situation and develop an appropriate response. If our worries are driven by our own insecurities and feelings of inadequacy, we can develop renewed self-confidence by doing what is necessary to correct the problem, sharpen our skills, and improve our performance.

18. WORRY WILL KILL YOU QUICKER THAN WORK.

Worry is perhaps the most useless of all human activities. As humorist Will Rogers once observed, "Worry is like a rocking chair. It keeps you busy, but it doesn't get you anywhere." Worry does not solve anything; it only serves to place additional pressure upon you. If there is such a thing as constructive worry, it would be taking a positive approach to potential problems by anticipating them before they occur and developing alternative solutions to them. If you are faced with a problem that might evolve in several different directions, for example, try developing a decision tree with a plan of action for each eventuality. When you have a carefully planned response for every possible problem, you won't have to waste your time in unproductive, unnecessary worry.

19. NEVER LISTEN TO A DOUBTING THOMAS UNLESS YOU ARE WILLING TO BECOME ONE, FOR DOUBT IS CONTAGIOUS.

We human beings have a great capacity for doubt. Despite our most valiant efforts to overcome our doubts and insecurities, they occasionally creep into our minds before we realize what is happening. A negative word from another may be enough to trigger our own suppressed negative feelings and unleash a wave of groundless fears. Positive thinking is something that is learned, fragile, and usually countercultural. It must be practiced constantly.

20. MOST WORRIES ARE NOT HALF AS SERIOUS AS WE FIRST THINK THEY ARE.

Many a night's sleep has been lost over worries that become inconsequential when exposed to the bright light of a new day. Things always seem bleakest in the dark of night or when we are all alone. At such times, the mind has a way of exaggerating the circumstances until we convince ourselves that things are far worse than they actually are. Don't waste energy in needless worry that could be directed toward solving the problem.

If you have trouble sleeping because your worries keep you awake, try keeping a notepad beside your bed. Instead of worrying about something you must do, or fretting about a problem you are unsure how to solve, make a list of the things you should do tomorrow to address the situation. You will find that it's much easier to leave your worries on the pad than turning them over and over in your mind throughout the night.

21. IF YOU ARE TOO BUSY TO SPEND TIME WITH WORRIES, THEY'LL BE TOO DISCOURAGED TO HANG AROUND.

Worry is a companion like any other—it won't stay around for long if you don't spend time with it. When you are so busy with positive, constructive actions that you don't have time to worry, you have already begun to climb the ladder of success.

This is not to suggest that you should blithely ignore problems. What it does mean is that you should not so internalize problems that you are paralyzed and unable to take constructive action. When you find that your worries are keeping you awake at night, remember the cracker-barrel wisdom that the best way to kill your worries is to work them to death.

22. IF I HAD BUT ONE WISH AND IT COULD BE GRANTED FOR THE ASKING, I WOULD ASK FOR MORE WISDOM WITH WHICH TO ENJOY THE MANY BLESSINGS I POSSESS UNDER THE AMERICAN FORM OF GOVERNMENT.

Someone once said that democracy is a lot like making sausage. It's not very pretty, but the result is all that matters. We are indeed fortunate that our country's founders were learned and had themselves experienced oppression. They were determined to construct a system of democracy that would allow an open and honest analysis of public policy, which would ultimately lead us to decisions that best serve the majority of the people.

We are blessed with a model of democracy and free-market economics that other countries around the world can only strive to emulate. The next time you're involved in a conversation in which others criticize our form of government, put in a good word for America. Remind them how fortunate we are to live in a country where we can openly criticize our leaders, argue among ourselves, and ultimately arrive at a solution that best serves us all.

23. FAITH CANNOT BE CREATED, BUT IT CAN BE APPROPRIATED BY ALL WHO HAVE PREPARED THEIR MINDS TO RECEIVE IT.

In some religions, it is called the "gift of faith," a gift from God to those who are mentally prepared to receive it. When you accept the existence of faith, even though it cannot be explained by logical, rational thought, you will begin to receive its benefits. When you develop the capacity for faith, you will experience a wonderful sense of contentment and well-being that comes from the knowledge that a Higher Power is available to you whenever you need it.

You exercise faith when you practice your religion, accepting the doctrine of your church, synagogue, or mosque—even though the existence of God cannot be proven empirically. You also exhibit faith when you trust another to deliver on his or her promises in a business deal, and you demonstrate your faith in yourself every time you attempt to do something you have never done before.

24. FAITH NEVER DIMINISHES THROUGH USE, BUT IT INCREASES THEREBY.

Like your body and mind, your faith becomes stronger when you exercise it. The first time you "take the leap of faith," you may be understandably apprehensive. It is not easy to accept an abstract idea as fact, or to attempt something when you are unsure of the outcome. When you apply your faith, however, you will find that if your cause is just and you have faith in God, in other people, and in yourself, you will achieve what you desire.

You will experience moments of uncertainty when you are unsure of yourself and what action you should take. When you do, trust your instincts. It does not matter whether your intuition comes from Infinite Intelligence or whether it is the sum of your knowledge and experience. The important thing to remember is that the power is yours to be used.

25. THE GREATEST OF ALL MIRACLES IS THE POWER OF SIMPLE FAITH.

Because faith is an essential element of Christianity, the New Testament is filled with references to the power of faith. In the book of Matthew, Jesus told the unbelievers that if they but had "faith as a grain of mustard seed," they would have the power to move mountains, and with faith nothing would be impossible for them. In the book of Mark, He told the faithful that "all things *are* possible to him that believeth." In biblical teachings, faith is "the substance of things hoped for, the evidence of things not seen." In short, faith is the active expression of a willingness to believe in that which we cannot prove. It is indeed a miracle.

26. FEAR IS THE MOST COSTLY OF ALL THE HUMAN EMOTIONS EVEN THOUGH MOST FEARS HAVE NO FOUNDATION IN FACT.

The greatest enemies of success are indecision, doubt, and fear. As long as you are plagued by doubts and fears, you will be indecisive, and indecision is the seedling of fear. It crystallizes into doubt, and the two combine to create fear. These enemies are especially dangerous because they germinate slowly and grow unobserved.

Seven basic fears can stand between you and success. They are the fear of: poverty, criticism, ill health, loss of love, liberty, old age, and death. Because your mind always seeks to transform your thoughts into their physical equivalent, you must use your absolute power over what you think to eliminate such negative impulses and replace them with positive thoughts. By mastering your thoughts, you master your fears.

27. GO TO BED PRAYING AND GET UP SINGING, AND NOTICE WHAT A FINE DAY'S WORK YOU WILL DO.

Religion is particularly helpful in placing human existence in perspective and in developing the proper attitude to acquire the blessings of life for yourself and your family. By using the power of prayer to connect with the Supreme Being, you learn to trust your nobler instincts and enable your spiritual growth. When you express gratitude for your blessings every night and welcome each new day with a song, you will be able to deal with whatever life throws at you.

28. WOULD YOU TAKE A CHANCE ON BEING JUDGED IN HEAVEN BY THE SAME RULES YOU USE TO JUDGE YOUR FELLOW MEN?

How easy it is to have one set of rules for ourselves and another for everyone else. One of the most profound biblical concepts is the admonition to walk a mile in another's shoes before criticizing him or her. When you are tempted to be critical of a colleague or a family member, pause for a moment and ask yourself: How do I measure up? Am I criticizing this person for behavior I sometimes exhibit myself? Just because they are not doing things the way I would, does it mean they are wrong? You may find that when you seriously consider another's approach, you will learn a better way to do things yourself.

29. HOPE AND FEAR DON'T TRAVEL TOGETHER.

Hope and fear are conflicting emotions; as long as you have hope, you can overcome whatever fears assail you. Hope gives you the courage to persevere in the face of adversity, to seek new frontiers of achievement. As psychiatrist and author Karl Menninger said, "Hope is modest, humble, selfless; it implies progress; it is an adventure, a going forward—a confident search for a rewarding life."

Hope is the outgrowth of preparation. When you examine the possibilities in a spirit of positive achievement, hope is the inevitable result. If you take the appropriate steps to prepare yourself for success in any endeavor, you will acquire the self-confidence that will lead you surely and swiftly to the object of your desire. When you experience delays, setbacks, and temporary defeats, hope gives you the courage to persist until you overcome the doubts and fears that plague us all from time to time.

30. LIFE NEVER IS SWEET TO THOSE WHO ARE SOURED ON THE WORLD.

You can expect to benefit from life in direct proportion to what you invest in it. If you plant positive thoughts and deeds, you will reap a bountiful harvest. But if you sow hatred and discontent, you can expect to receive the same result in kind. When you grudgingly give only what you must, you must expect that you will receive in return only what others are forced to give to you.

You may consciously choose to be a positive, considerate,

active achiever who makes things happen, or you may choose to wait, watch, and grow old and bitter. Sadly, when you allow yourself to flounder in negativism, you may not realize the harm you've done until it is too late. When you choose to be happy and successful, you will find happiness and success, but you needn't choose negativism and failure. It will find you on its own.

31. ONLY ONE THING WILL ATTRACT LOVE, AND THAT IS LOVE.

Love is one of life's great mysteries. It is impossible to explain the rapture you feel when you experience love, and words alone cannot describe the intensity of emotion that engulfs you when you connect mentally and physically with another human being. And how can you express the indescribable feeling that accompanies holding your own child for the very first time? Such is the dominion of love.

Like friendship, you cannot receive true love unless you are first willing to give it. Love always involves risk. When you extend your love to another, you do so in the hope that your love will be accepted and returned in an equal measure. But unless you are willing to give of yourself first, you will never know the joy that comes from receiving unqualified, generous, understanding love. You may be hurt if you love too much, but you will live in misery if you love too little.

CREDITS

NAPOLEON HILL was born in a one-room cabin on the Pound River in Wise County, Virginia. He began his writing career at thirteen years of age as a "mountain reporter" for small-town newspapers and was the first American author to publish an organized philosophy of personal achievement. He went on to become the bestselling motivational author of all time. His book, *Think and Grow Rich*, has sold more than 20 million copies and has been translated into several languages. He died in South Carolina in 1970 at the age of eighty-seven.

W. CLEMENT STONE is an insurance tycoon and philanthropist, who was a business partner with Napoleon Hill. Mr. Stone is coauthor with Napoleon Hill of the book *Success Through a Positive Mental Attitude*, and author of the book *Success System That Never Fails*. Mr. Stone is president of the Napoleon Hill Foundation.

MICHAEL J. RITT, JR., was secretary and office manager to Napoleon Hill from 1952 through 1962 and is currently secretary, treasurer, and executive director of the Napoleon Hill Foundation. Mr. Ritt is also writer and creator of Napoleon Hill audiotapes, motivational products, calendars, books, courses, and *Think and Grow Rich Newsletter*.

SAMUEL A. CYPERT is editor and publisher of *Think and Grow Rich Newsletter*, a monthly newsletter based upon the principles of success that Napoleon Hill wrote about in his bestselling books. He is author of several books on personal achievement, including *Believe and Achieve: W. Clement Stone's Seventeen Principles of Success*, *The Success Break-*

through, and *The Power of Self-Esteem*. He began his writing career as editor of a weekly newspaper in his home state of Oklahoma and today lives with his family in Birmingham, Michigan.

Upon request, the reader may receive an autographed bookplate bearing the signature of Napoleon Hill. Address your request to the Napoleon Hill Foundation, 1440 Paddock Drive, Northbrook, IL 60062, and enclose a large, self-addressed, stamped envelope. With this bookplate, you will receive a copy of one of Dr. Hill's famous essays on success.

DUTTON **PLUME**

THE LATEST WORDS ON BUSINESS

☐ **WINNIE-THE-POOH ON PROBLEM SOLVING** *In which Pooh, Piglet and friends explore How to Solve Problems so you can too* **by Roger E. Allen and Stephen D. Allen.** Using the well-known adventures of Pooh and friends, this book teaches and explains the unique SOLVE Problem-Solving Method, a step-by-step system of identifying, analyzing, and resolving problems. Pooh, and you, learn all the principles of practical problem solving, which can be applied as easily to the many challenges that are part of today's rapidly changing and complex world. (940631—$17.95)

☐ **WINNIE-THE-POOH ON MANAGEMENT** *In which a Very Important Bear and his friends are introduced to a Very Important Subject* **by Roger E. Allen.** Using the characters and the stories of A.A. Milne to illustrate such principles as setting clear objectives, strong leadership, the need for accurate information, good communication, and other neglected basics of prudent management, the author offers sensible, time-honored advice in a captivating style.

(938982—$17.95)

☐ **FROM HERE TO ECONOMY** *A Shortcut to Economic Literacy.* **by Todd G. Buchholz.** With refreshing wit and irreverence, the author takes readers by the hand and reveals the basic rules behind everything from food prices to trade deficits. He gives us a precise and accessible understanding of economic ideas, actions, and consequences as they actually exist in the here and now.

(939024—$21.95)

☐ **JUNGLE RULES** *How to Be a Tiger in Business* **by John P. Imlay, Jr., with Dennis Hamilton.** This compelling guide is not only about how to be a great manager yourself but how to build a great management team—picking the brightest and best and empowering them to conquer new territories on their own. All of the authors techniques are designed to enable people to be movers and shakers. "A must read for anyone who puts customers first and has the drive to succeed in a dynamic marketplace."—Harvey Mackay (271754—$13.95)

Prices slightly higher in Canada.

PLUME **DUTTON**

MOVING UP

(0452)

☐ **NAPOLEON HILL'S KEYS TO SUCCESS** *The 17 Principles of Personal Achievement.* Anyone seeking personal and financial improvement will find invaluable mental exercises, self-analysis techniques, powerful encouragement, and straightforward advice in this illuminating guide. In addition to Hill's many personal true-life examples, there are also contemporary illustrations featuring dynamos like Bill Gates, Peter Lynch, and Donna Karan. (938869—$21.95)

☐ **NAPOLEON HILL'S A YEAR OF GROWING RICH** *52 Steps to Achieving Life's Rewards.* **Foreword by W. Clement Stone.** An inspiring . . . empowering work. You'll learn to realize all the strengths within you and spot the vast wealth of opportunities at your fingertips. (270545—$10.95)

☐ **TIME MANAGEMENT MADE EASY by Peter Turla and Kathleen L. Hawkins.** Revolutionize the way you manage time with this easy-to-use program for increasing your personal productivity without working harder or longer. It shows you exactly how to focus on high-payoff activities and eliminate time-wasting behavior and procrastination. (272025—$15.95)

Prices slightly higher in Canada.